NATIONAL
GEOGRAPHIC
KiDS

ANiMAL JAM

OFFiCiAL iNSiDER'S GUiDE

2ND EDITION

KATHERiNE NOLL

NATIONAL GEOGRAPHIC
WASHINGTON, D.C.

TABLE OF CONTENTS

Welcome to ANiMaL JaM!

Get ready to play wild in the amazing online virtual playground of Animal Jam, created especially for kids who love animals.

ANIMAL JAM AND NATIONAL GEOGRAPHIC KIDS HAVE TEAMED UP to bring you a fun, exciting, and safe environment to play in online, but also to inspire you to explore and protect the natural world outside your doors. In this live, multiplayer, online playground, you will travel to the land of Jamaa to play games, meet new friends, and explore distant lands, all while learning cool stuff about animals, plants, habitats, and more. So get ready to dig into an ancient rain forest ruin, learn what it's like to be part of a wolf pack, dive into the deepest depths of the ocean, and climb the highest mountain peak on your adventure!

This book is your guide to everything Animal Jam has to offer. You'll also get an insider's look at Jamaa and come away with tips and tricks on everything from shopping to games and even learn how Jamaa was created.

Every time you see the National Geographic yellow border you'll be provided amazing info on some of the coolest places around the world. You will soon discover that the fictional world of Jamaa isn't so different from our own planet! So come meet over 75 million Animal Jam players, or Jammers. Welcome, and get ready for an exciting Jamaa journey.

Let Peck be your guide to Animal Jam!

Peck appears throughout this book to share her advice and tips with all Jammers. Can you find all the places she appears inside? Look closely and count every Peck you see. Then head to animaljam.com, log in to your account, and click "I Have a Code to Enter!" Spell out the number of Pecks you've counted (e.g., 2 = two) to earn a special prize!

THE RULES

THERE ARE RULES EVERYWHERE TO KEEP PEOPLE SAFE.

When you're riding in a car, you have to put your seat belt on. If you're riding a bike, you wear a helmet. Even extreme sports—like bungee jumping and skydiving—are done with strict safety guidelines.

Going on the Internet is no different. There are rules you need to follow to keep yourself and others safe. Animal Jam and its creators are committed to providing a safe environment so everyone can have a fun gaming experience. Here are four tips you should always remember online, whether you're on Animal Jam or any other website.

PLAY WILD, PLAY SAFE

1. BE VERY CAREFUL WHO YOU SHARE YOUR PERSONAL INFORMATION WITH, LIKE YOUR REAL NAME AND AGE.
Keep your contact info, like your phone number and home and email addresses, private. Only share when your parents say it's okay to share.

2. NEVER GIVE ANYONE YOUR PASSWORD.
Passwords for any sites, not just Animal Jam, should be kept to yourself and your parents. People online might promise to give you cool stuff if you give them your password. Don't believe them. It's a trick!

3. NEVER MEET ANYONE IN PERSON WHO YOU MET ON THE INTERNET.
Sometimes people aren't who they say they are online.

4. BE NICE TO EVERYONE.
Do you like having fun on Animal Jam? We do too! Let's keep it a happy place by being nice to everyone. When people are mean or bully each other, it makes the Internet less fun. So do your part and always be friendly.

Follow these rules online to stay safe and keep having a good time! For more information on Animal Jam's safety and privacy policies, grab a parent and check out animaljam.com/rules and animaljam.com/privacy.

THE DAWN OF THE ALPHAS

Today the world of Jamaa is home to millions of animals living in peace. Yet a long time ago, this wonderful world was nearly lost!

JAMAA WAS ONCE HOME TO HUNDREDS OF ANIMAL species of all shapes and sizes. These animals spent their days playing games, going to parties, building homes, and living together as friends.

Mira and Zios, the guardian spirits of Jamaa, gifted each animal species with a Heartstone, a special jewel that contained the essence and secrets of that species.

Read the story behind the world of **ANIMAL JAM!**

For many generations, all the Heartstones were kept together in a vault beneath the Lost Temple of Zios. Every animal could visit them and see the unique gifts that each species brought to Jamaa.

UNREST IN JAMAA

BUT AS TIME PASSED, THINGS CHANGED. ANIMALS began to fear and mistrust other species. Some animals stopped living together as a united community. Soon all the feelings of friendship in Jamaa were gone, and the animals built new villages for their kind only. Koalas lived and talked only with other koalas. So did rhinos. And crocodiles. Before long, all the animals in Jamaa stopped working together to make Jamaa a happy and vibrant place. Worst of all, many animal species took their Heartstones from the Lost Temple of Zios and hid them in their new villages.

It was during this time of division that the dark Phantoms first appeared.

RISE OF THE PHANTOMS

THE PHANTOMS CAME THROUGH DARK PORTALS, AND they quickly spread through the uninhabited regions of Jamaa. Wherever the Phantoms went, they left a trail of spoiling destruction. Rivers were polluted, trees became bare, and the air was thick with noxious fumes. The Phantoms consumed everything in the environment and gave nothing back. They leveled entire villages the animals had built and left the entire civilization in pieces.

LIZA
PANDA

Liza's face is a familiar one to all Jammers. Liza's always been a traveler and explorer. When she was first called as an Alpha, it was a very different place. Not only were the Phantoms wreaking havoc, but also none of the animal species that lived in Jamaa got along with one another. Liza's talent as a peacemaker helped bring the animals together again.

Calm and friendly, Liza is always eager to help other animals out. That is, when she's not taking photos all around Jamaa. It's her favorite thing to do!

Named after Eliza Scidmore (1856–1928), a journalist, photographer, world traveler, and the first woman to serve on the National Geographic board.

Because animals were spread out in isolated villages, the Phantoms easily conquered these villages one by one. The animals soon discovered that if the Phantoms reached a Heartstone, they could imprison the animals of that species inside it! Each time the Phantoms captured a Heartstone, an entire species disappeared from Jamaa.

Mira and Zios watched in horror as the Phantoms spread throughout Jamaa. As guardian spirits, it hurt them to see the land they loved become corrupted, and they knew they could bring Jamaa back to life if the Phantoms were repelled. In time, they could make the skies and waters clear again, and if they could recover the lost Heartstones, thousands of animals could return to Jamaa. As time drew on, however, the Phantom threat grew only more fearsome and unstoppable.

TaKiNG a StaND

REMEMBERING HOW MUCH THEY HAD ACCOMPLISHED when they lived and worked together, the remaining six species gathered their Heartstones, left their villages, and returned to the Lost Temple of Zios. As the tigers, monkeys, koalas, pandas, bunnies, and wolves of Jamaa gathered together for one last stand against the Phantoms, Mira and Zios saw that it would not be enough.

In desperation, the guardian spirits of Jamaa searched for animals who could lead their species.

THe ALPHaS

GraHaM

MONKEY

Named after Alexander Graham Bell (1847–1922), inventor of the telephone and second president of the National Geographic Society.

Graham thinks the other Alphas always do things the hard way. For example, Liza once tracked a Heartstone to a Phantom cavern sealed by an enormous boulder. By the time Graham got there, Liza had dozens of animals straining to move the stone, but it wouldn't budge.

For Graham, it was the simplest thing in the world to build a waterwheel using a system of gears, pulleys, and counterweights. With the pull of a lever, the gigantic rock moved with ease! Broken gadgets and gizmos are quickly fixed when Graham handles them. Is it magic, science, or simply extraordinary luck? The other Alphas aren't sure, but they like the amazing results Graham achieves.

THE ALPHAS

Before Cosmo was called as an Alpha, he seemed to be a fairly typical koala: He spent most of his time in trees, eating leaves and napping. But even then, there was always something different about Cosmo: He understood plants.

Cosmo knows what plants are saying—to each other, to animals, and sometimes even to themselves. The plants in Jamaa talk to Cosmo and tell him how to create potions with hundreds of uses.

As the youngest of the Alphas, Cosmo and Peck are always joking around. But there's one thing Cosmo never jokes about. He has a deep respect for the power of the natural world, perhaps because he is able to communicate with so much of it.

COSMO
KOALA

Named after the Cosmos Club, a private club in Washington, D.C., where the first ever meeting of the National Geographic Society took place in 1888.

They finally found six extraordinary leaders: Sir Gilbert the regal tiger, Cosmo the knowledgeable koala, Graham the inventive monkey, Greely the mysterious wolf, Liza the curious panda, and Peck the creative bunny. These were six remarkable animals with different personalities, but they were united in their strength of character and their respect for the natural world.

Mira and Zios chose well, and these very different animals soon formed a family.

To help in the battle against the Phantoms, Mira and Zios gave the new leaders Alpha Stones, six special jewels that harnessed the Alphas' abilities and the natural powers of Jamaa. With these stones, the six chosen animals became Alphas, the heroes chosen to save Jamaa in its darkest hour!

The Alphas set about making a plan that utilized each of their unique abilities to defeat the Phantoms. Once the plan was finalized, they joined the rest of the animals who had gathered together to face the flood of Phantoms before them. When the animals saw the magnificent Alphas, they felt their own bravery return. The Alphas felt strength flowing through them, and with many roars, howls, and cheers, they all stormed into battle.

The Fight to Save Jamaa

THE BATTLE FOR JAMAA WAS EPIC, WITH THE ANIMALS and Alphas fighting not just for themselves, but also for the beautiful land that Jamaa once was. Animals that were once scared of the Phantoms found new courage, and animals that had shunned and despised others worked side by side with different species.

As the animals marched forward, the Phantoms escaped by fleeing into their dark portals. But just as the last of the Phantoms were retreating, they overtook Zios and vanished with him into a portal. Mira quickly dove into a dark portal, following Zios and the Phantoms, disappearing as the portal closed.

The sudden absence of Zios and Mira was a tragic blow to the animals. Despite their sadness, they realized that for the first time many of them could remember, Jamaa was free of the Phantoms!

THE ALPHAS

Peck is noisy and excitable, but Mira also saw a creative problem-solver in her. Peck is a musician and a talented artist who has done much to beautify the world. She inspires all the animals in Jamaa to explore their creative side and join her in art projects.

Have you ever had a friend who seemed to be made out of pure energy, who could never sit still, and who was always trying to involve you in some new, crazy scheme? That's Peck! She moves in a blur, gets bored easily, and never seems to run out of ideas. She takes her role as a mentor to other animals very seriously, though, and she is determined to get Jamaa's animals into shape and ready for whatever the Phantoms might throw at them.

PECK
BUNNY
Named after Annie Smith Peck (1850–1935), a record-setting mountain climber and explorer.

REBUILDING THEIR HOME

JAMAA HAD BEEN SAVED, BUT THE DAMAGE THE Phantoms had caused was everywhere. Plants and trees were sick, clouds of poison smoke hung in the air, and the land itself was littered with burnt plastic refuse that seemed to follow the Phantoms wherever they went. The Alphas knew it would be the responsibility of every animal in Jamaa, including themselves, to return the land to its former glory.

While the animals worked hard to rebuild, cleansing power from the Alpha Stones flowed through the Alphas and into the land. Soon, the rivers were running clear, the trees regained their leaves, and the air was fresh and crisp. The pristine beauty of Jamaa had spread from the top of Mt. Shiveer to the bottom of Deep Blue.

During this time, Peck stayed in Jamaa Township to protect the village and help new animals that came to Jamaa, while the other Alphas separated to explore lost lands and track the Phantoms to their source. They were able to restore many of the lands that had been taken over by the Phantoms, and many Heartstones were returned. Animals trapped inside the Heartstones were freed to return to their homes, and they were welcomed by all their animal friends. In a short time, the world of Jamaa began to resemble the beautiful world it once was.

THE ALPHAS

GREELY
WOLF

Named after Adolphus Greely (1844–1935), Arctic explorer and a founding member of the National Geographic Society.

Solitary by nature and a master of stealth, Greely spends most of his time alone and far from Jamaa, observing the movements of the Phantoms and sabotaging them from the shadows. These movements make many animals very nervous; it sometimes seems as though Greely can appear anywhere, anytime.

Some of the other Alphas don't trust Greely and his methods, but they certainly respect him. He knows more about the Phantoms and their movements than anyone, and it's possible the Phantoms fear him more than any of the other Alphas.

THE ALPHAS

Ever since he was a cub, Sir Gilbert wondered what it must be like to be a monkey. Or a giraffe. Or a penguin, shark, or rabbit. All other animals fascinate him!

Sir Gilbert's favorite thing about being an Alpha is socializing with many different kinds of animals. He's impeccably polite, quietly dignified, and sensibly cautious. Sometimes the other Alphas tease Sir Gilbert about his regal manners, but everyone respects the noble tiger.

SIR GILBERT
TIGER

Named after Gilbert H. Grosvenor (1875–1966), a writer and geographer who not only became the first full-time editor of National Geographic magazine but served as president of the National Geographic Society, too.

A LASTING PEACE?

MILLIONS OF ANIMALS NOW LIVE IN PEACE AND happiness in Jamaa. The Alphas continue to explore new lands, and whenever they are able to drive the Phantoms out of an area or reclaim a Heartstone, the animals of Jamaa celebrate that they have new lands to play in and new animal friends to play with!

Many years have passed since all of Jamaa was nearly lost, but now some of the Phantoms have returned, and they are once again trying to ruin the peace and joy of Jamaa.

Read on to find out the best tips and tricks to help the animals of Jamaa rid their land of Phantoms forever!

Buddies

Jamaa Journal

Parties

Gems

Mail

Jammer Wall

Journey Book

Games

GETTING STARTED
in ANIMAL JAM
AND
ANIMAL JAM –
PLAY WILD!

ANIMAL JAM— at your DESK, OR ON THE GO!

NO MATTER WHAT DEVICE you're using, there are lots of ways to visit the world of Jamaa. Head to animaljam.com or play on your mobile device through the Animal Jam – Play Wild! app.

Change Your Look

Switch Animals

Actions

Chat

Emotes

Username

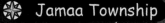 Jamaa Township

Location

Report a Player

#1 Pick Your Animal and Name
Choose from a set of animals and create a name as unique as you are.

#2 Fill Out Your Info
Enter your information, then create a unique username and password. Be sure to ask a parent if you need help!

#3 Get the Look
Follow Peck to learn the basics, customize your look, and get some free stuff! Then head into Jamaa to play wild!

#4 You're ready to play!
In Animal Jam, there is so much to do and so many things to explore! Read the Jamaa Journal to learn all about the newest features to come to Jamaa, and don't forget to check out the Daily Explorer, Animal Jam's official blog, at blog.animaljam.com.

Den

World Map

Chat Bar

Volume

Discover ANIMAL JAM – PLAY WILD!

At HOME or ON tHE GO, tHERE'S SO MUCH to EXPLORE iN tHE MOBiLE VERSiON OF ANiMAL JAM!

THERE'S MORE THAN ONE WAY TO VISIT JAMAA, WHICH MAKES the fun almost endless! Animal Jam – Play Wild! is the super-cool mobile version of the game that has tons of the fun of Animal Jam, plus a few unique surprises. Read on to learn more and prepare to journey to Jamaa wherever and whenever you want!

The Look
Play Wild! is an entirely 3-D world, so you can see all the amazing and lush details of Jamaa come to life.

Currency

In Play Wild!, Jammers use Sapphires to purchase incredible dens, pets, accessories, den items, and tons more awesome stuff. Learn more about all the cool currencies of Jamaa on pages 38–39.

Dens, Games, and Pets

Jammers can buy awesome dens, adopt adorable pets, and play cool games only available on Animal Jam – Play Wild! Check out pages 32–33 to learn more about dens, pages 62–67 for more about pets, and pages 256–261 for a list of games you can play.

Treasure Hunts

X marks the spot! In Play Wild!, you can go on Treasure Hunts every day to win Gems, items, and even Sapphires. Which treasure chests hold the treasure? Unlock them to find out!

ALPHA TIP   COSMO

There's lots more fun to discover in Play Wild!, like fun parties, secret areas only for certain animals, awesome items and accessories, and tons of fun that's yet to come!

EXPLORE

Mt. Shiveer

Jamaa Township

Appondale

Kimbara Outback

World Map

IF YOU'RE LOOKING TO explore Jamaa, all you need to do is decide where you want to go and click that area of the map! It's that easy. You'll find the World Map on the bottom right-hand corner of the screen. Each land in Jamaa is full of fantastic facts, fun games, and interesting sites to see and play in.

You can also find all of the cool shops and theaters of Jamaa by using the buttons on the right side of your screen.

If you want to go exploring and brave the wilds without a map, you can walk or swim from place to place. To delve into the oceans, you'll need an ocean animal. And if you want to explore the skies, you'll need a flying animal. Look for the wave icon in the Add Animal menu for an animal that can help you explore the ocean depths; to soar through the skies, choose a flying animal.

JaMaa!

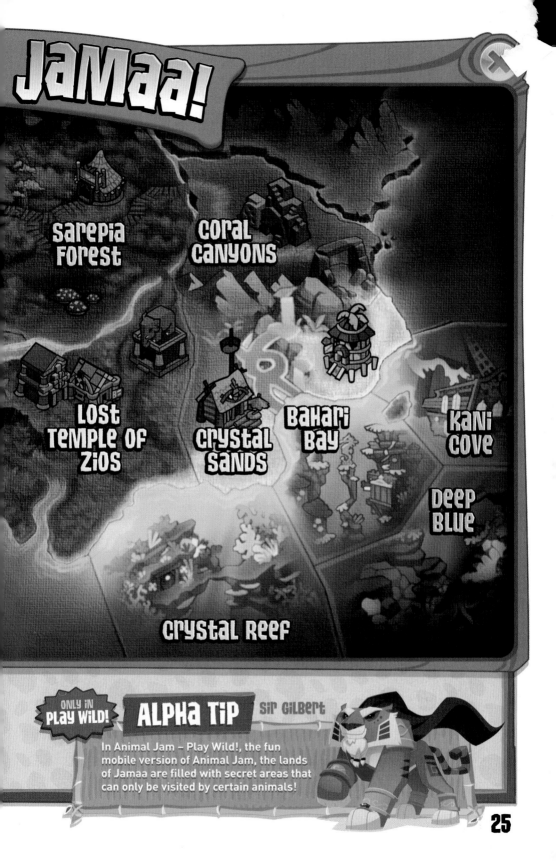

SAREPIA FOREST

CORAL CANYONS

LOST TEMPLE OF ZIOS

CRYSTAL SANDS

BAHARI BAY

KANI COVE

DEEP BLUE

CRYSTAL REEF

ALPHA TIP   Sir Gilbert

In Animal Jam – Play Wild!, the fun mobile version of Animal Jam, the lands of Jamaa are filled with secret areas that can only be visited by certain animals!

BECOME YOUR Favorite ANiMaL!

IN JaMaa, you caN Play as your Favorite aNiMaL—But that's NOt aLL!

YOU CAN ALSO CUSTOMIZE YOUR ANIMAL WITH DIFFERENT COLORS, EYES, PATTERNS, AND clothing, making a creature that's totally unique and yours alone.

From time to time, you'll notice some of the animal species in Jamaa are traveling or exploring, which means you cannot choose them when making a new animal. In the wild, animals travel for lots of different reasons. Sometimes they are searching for food, looking for warmer weather, or just hoping for a change of scenery! Just like wild animals, the species in Jamaa will sometimes decide to go traveling or exploring, too. Don't worry: They always come back. You'll just have to wait until they return to Jamaa!

Check out all the animals living in Jamaa as of now. Since the Alphas are always searching for lost Heartstones, new species are discovered all the time!

Arctic Fox

Scamper in the snow as an arctic fox!

Arctic foxes use their long, fluffy tails as a blanket! *Turn to page 232 to learn more about arctic foxes.*

Arctic Wolf

Prowl through the tundra as an arctic wolf!

These white wolves are sub-species of gray wolves, but they have smaller ears and muzzles to better preserve body heat. *Turn to page 130 to learn more about arctic wolves.*

Bunny

As a bunny, you'll be the hoppiest animal in Jamaa!

Rabbits have almost twice as many taste buds on their tongues as humans do. *Turn to page 82 to learn more about bunnies.*

Cheetah

Zoom around Jamaa as the fastest land animal in the world.

Cheetah cubs have a mane on their neck and shoulders that looks like a mini-mohawk! *Turn to page 110 to learn more about cheetahs.*

Cougar

Pounce like a pro on the rocks of Coral Canyons!

All cougar kittens are born with blue eyes. *Turn to page 158 to learn more about cougars.*

Coyote

Sing along with the pack's yowling song!

Coyotes are sometimes called prairie or brush wolves. *Turn to page 155 to learn more about coyotes.*

Crocodile

Everyone will wonder what you're smiling about.

When crocs sit with their mouths wide open revealing their sharp teeth, they're not trying to be scary. That's how they sweat! *Turn to page 118 to learn more about crocodiles.*

Deer

Leap around Sarepia Forest as a graceful deer.

The largest member of the deer species are moose. *Turn to page 134 to learn more about deer.*

Dolphin

Flip for joy in Bahari Bay as a dolphin.

Dolphins can swim up to five times faster than the fastest swimming human and dive as deep as 2,000 feet (610 m). *Turn to page 166 to learn more about dolphins.*

Eagle

Get a bird's-eye view of all of Jamaa as you soar high above.

It's tough for eagles to super-size their dinner. These carnivorous birds can lift only about half of their body weight! *Turn to page 224 to learn more about eagles.*

Elephant

As an elephant, you'll never forget all the cool things there are to do in Jamaa!

Elephants can eat 300 pounds (136 kg) of food in one day! *Turn to page 114 to learn more about elephants.*

Falcon

Love to zoom, swoop, and soar? A falcon may strike your fancy!

Peregrine falcons can dive at up to 200 miles an hour (320 km/h)! *Turn to page 154 to learn more about falcons.*

Flamingo

Bold, bright, and beautiful, the colorful flamingo knows how to make a splash!

Flamingos can eat only when their heads are upside down. *Turn to page 181 to learn more about flamingos.*

Fox

As a quick fox you can jump over any lazy animals who might be in your way!

In legends and fairy tales, foxes are often described as cunning, magical creatures. *Turn to page 151 to learn more about foxes.*

When you see this symbol it means the animal **CAN TRAVEL IN JAMAA'S OCEANS.**

When you see this symbol it means the animal **CAN TRAVEL IN JAMAA'S SKIES.**

Giraffe

Reach new heights in Appondale as a giraffe.

You might sleep with your head on a comfy pillow, but giraffes almost always sleep standing up! *Turn to page 117 to learn more about giraffes.*

Goat

Live on the edge as a sure-footed goat!

The pupils in the eyes of goats are shaped like rectangles. *Turn to page 87 to learn more about goats.*

Horse

Race to the finish line in the Jamaa Derby as a horse.

Surround sound! Because they can rotate their ears 180 degrees, horses have excellent hearing. *Turn to page 159 to learn more about horses.*

Hyena

Laugh it up on the savannas of Appondale as a hyena.

Spotted hyenas make a laugh-like sound when nervous or excited! *Turn to page 122 to learn more about hyenas.*

Kangaroo

If you're feeling jumpy, go explore Kimbara Outback as a kangaroo.

In Australia, there are more kangaroos than people. *Turn to page 243 to learn more about kangaroos.*

Koala

Explore Jamaa as a cute and cuddly koala.

Koalas don't need to worry about bad breath. Their diet of eucalyptus leaves makes it smell like minty cough drops! *Turn to page 242 to learn more about koalas.*

Lemur

As a lemur, fun is only a leap, a swing, and a jump away!

Wild lemurs are primates that only live on the island of Madagascar. *Turn to page 123 to learn more about lemurs.*

Lion

You'll be the king or queen of Jamaa as this royal cat.

Lion prides can have as few as 3 members or as many as 30. *Turn to page 113 to learn more about lions.*

Llama

Pack up and climb high as a llama in Jamaa!

Llamas can carry heavy loads, but if they are packed with too much weight, they'll lie down and refuse to move until their burden is lessened. *Turn to page 83 to learn more about llamas.*

Lynx

Sneak about Jamaa with ease—this snowy cat knows how to keep its cover.

Lynxes use the tufts of hair on their ears to feel their way around—just like whiskers! *Turn to page 233 to learn more about lynxes.*

Monkey

If you want to monkey around, this is the animal for you.

They got their name for a reason. A group of howler monkeys can be heard up to three miles (5 km) away! *Turn to page 103 to learn more about monkeys.*

Octopus

You'll always have an extra helping hand if you pick this ocean animal.

If octopuses lose one of their eight arms, a new one grows back in its place! *Turn to page 214 to learn more about octopuses.*

Otter

Land or ocean? Get the best of both as an otter!

The sensitive whiskers around sea otters' mouths help them to detect fish. *Turn to page 180 to learn more about otters.*

Owl

Who-who-who's that? Jamaa's nocturnal favorite, the owl!

Owls have the best night vision of any animal. *Turn to page 138 to learn more about owls.*

Panda

What's black and white and adorable all over? A panda, of course!

Pandas spend most of their day eating—and going to the bathroom. Now that's one pet you wouldn't want to clean up after! *Turn to page 78 to learn more about pandas.*

Penguin

Put a little waddle in your walk as a penguin.

Penguins have their own unique voice, which helps them to find their mates or chicks in a crowd. *Turn to page 167 to learn more about penguins.*

Certain animals are available for Jammers who have purchased an **ANIMAL JAM MEMBERSHIP.** Once in a while, members-only animals are made available to all Jammers, so check often!

Pig

Prance around Jamaa as a playful pig! Playing in the mud is a must.

Potbellied pigs are great sniffers! Some law enforcement officers use them to sniff for clues. *Turn to page 86 to learn more about pigs.*

Polar Bear

You'll have a *brrr*-illiant time playing as a furry polar bear.

If you grew as fast as polar bears do, by the time you were a few months old you'd weigh over 100 pounds (45 kg)! *Turn to page 149 to learn more about polar bears.*

Raccoon

Only you will know what you're really thinking behind that mask!

High five! The tracks of raccoons are easy to identify: Their front paws have five toes, and the tracks look a lot like small human hands. *Turn to page 135 to learn more about raccoons.*

Red Panda

Neither bear nor raccoon, the adorable red panda is in a league of its own.

Red pandas' scientific name translates to "fire-colored cat." *Turn to page 139 to learn more about red pandas.*

Rhino

As a rhino you can charge right into the middle of all the action in Jamaa Township.

Adult rhinos have no natural predators except for humans. *Turn to page 115 to learn more about rhinos.*

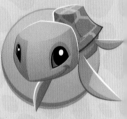

Sea Turtle

Strap on a shell and explore the sea!

The shells on sea turtles' backs are called carapaces, while the coverings on their bellies are called plastrons. *Turn to page 192 to learn more about sea turtles.*

Seal

Slippery seals glide gracefully under the waves!

Elephant seals can dive 5,000 feet (1,500 m) deep into the ocean and spend up to two hours at that depth. *Turn to page 172 to learn more about seals.*

Shark

My, what big teeth you have!

Instead of bone, sharks' skeletons are made mostly of cartilage—the material your nose and ears are made of. *Turn to page 204 to learn more about sharks.*

Sheep

Put a spring in your step as a sheep!

Sheep have four stomachs! *Turn to page 81 to learn more about sheep.*

Sloth

Slow and steady wins the race—especially when you're a sloth!

Three-toed sloths had a giant ancient cousin that was over 12 feet (4 m) tall! *Turn to page 98 to learn more about sloths.*

Snow Leopard

Ward off the chill in snowy Mt. Shiveer with a built-in fur coat!

Their strong legs enable snow leopards to leap as far as 50 feet (15 m) in one bound! *Turn to page 228 to learn more about snow leopards.*

Tiger

Sport some stylish stripes as a tiger.

Snack attack! Tigers don't eat only large prey animals like buffalo and deer. They'll also gobble up turtles and frogs. *Turn to page 94 to learn more about tigers.*

Toucan

Soar in style through Jamaa's skies as a colorful toucan.

Toucans' beaks are serrated like knives, so they can tear their meals apart and easily eat them. *Turn to page 99 to learn more about toucans.*

Wolf

Have a howling good time playing Animal Jam as a wolf!

Little Red Riding Hood got it wrong! Wolves almost never attack humans. The idea of the big bad wolf is a total fairy tale. *Turn to page 130 to learn more about wolves.*

ANIMAL DENS

ENCHANTED HOLLOW

JAMAALIDAY HOUSE

Whether it's a tree house, a restaurant, or a volcano, there's no place like home!

HOME IN ANIMAL JAM IS A DEN, BUT EACH den is as unique and different as the player who owns it. Animal Jam players get to show their personalities through their den decor. Always wanted to live underwater in a sunken ship? Or have a house filled with plushies? You can in Jamaa.

Den Sweet Den: Every Jammer starts off with the cozy Small House, and there are lots of additional dens to choose from.

Amazing Animal Architects

SO YOU THINK YOUR DECKED-OUT DEN IS pretty awesome? Wait until you see what these animals build in the wild!

Busy Beaver Builders

Beavers use their strong teeth and jaws to build their homes, called lodges, in large ponds.

Insect Skyscraper

In Africa, termites build their mounds up to 30 feet (9 m) high. They contain gardens, food storage areas, and cooling and ventilation systems!

Bowerbirds That Beautify!

Bowerbirds of New Guinea and Australia decorate their nests with everything from paint made from their own spit, to seashells, and even garlands made from caterpillar poop!

Personalize Your Den

If you're in a land den, you can shop for your den in the Jam Mart Furniture catalog. If you're in an ocean den, you'll see the Sunken Treasures catalog. You can pick out den items, floors, walls, toys, accessories, and more. Create a cool theme or pick out the items you like best—it's your choice.

Fantasy Castle

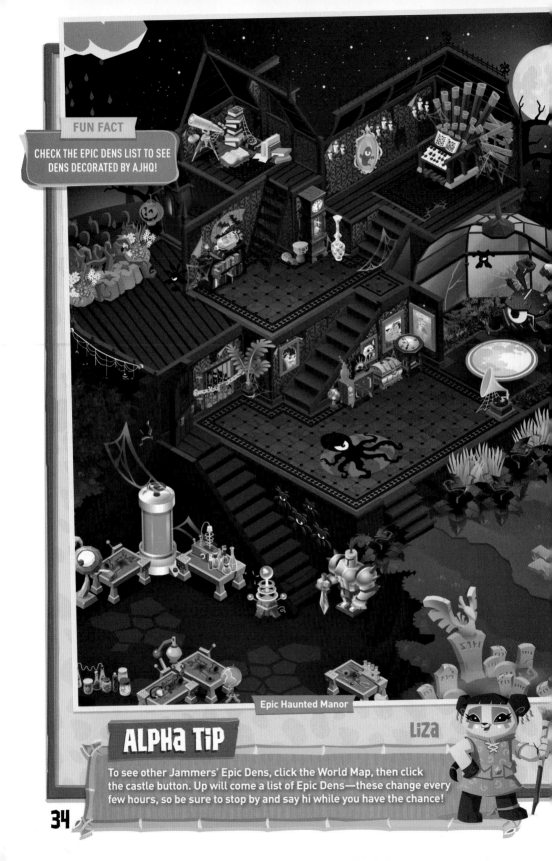

Epic Haunted Manor

ALPHA TIP

LiZa

To see other Jammers' Epic Dens, click the World Map, then click the castle button. Up will come a list of Epic Dens—these change every few hours, so be sure to stop by and say hi while you have the chance!

34

EPIC DENS

WANT TO GET NOTICED BY YOUR FELLOW JAMMERS?

YOU CAN! SIMPLY DECORATE YOUR DEN (OR DENS) WITH CARE, creativity, and commitment to design. Tailor your den so that it displays your own personal style—and Animal Jam HQ might just choose YOUR den to be on the Epic Dens list!

Here's how:

#1 Play games to win Gems, Diamonds, and Sapphires. Save your sparkling stones so that you can purchase the newest and coolest home furnishings, or even a new den!

#2 Every Jammer starts with their very own Small House. If you'd like to switch your den or get an additional one, you can use your Gems or Diamonds on AnimalJam.com, or Sapphires and Gems in Animal Jam – Play Wild! Visit the Diamond Shop, the Den Shop in Coral Canyons or Deep Blue, or simply click the "Switch Your Den" button while in your current den.

#3 Decorate your den to show off your unique flair. Dens can hold up to 300 items. There are so many awesome things to choose from—furniture, decorations, plants, games, wall items, even pets! The more colorful and inspired your den, the greater chance that you will catch the eye of AJHQ and get on the Epic Dens list.

#4 When your den is totally fabulous, unlock it so that other Jammers can check it out. If you want to increase your chances even more, throw a party! Invite your buddies, and visit other areas to spread the word. The more Jammers who come to your den, the more likely that it will get noticed.

Lucky Castle

Precious Happyflower

GreeLY

ALPHA TiP

Want to put a different spin on your Masterpieces? Use the Pixel Painting tool to create the coolest pixel art in Jamaa!

Create a
Masterpiece!

Bring your amazing artwork to Life!

DO YOU LOVE TO MAKE ART? GO TO CORAL Canyons to visit the Art Studio, where you'll find the perfect colors and tools for any aspiring artist! Choose among the paintbrush, air brush, paint bucket, paw smudge, and a variety of shapes to bring your vision to life on the blank canvas. Then, once your creation is complete, you can print it, save it, or even buy a frame for it and hang it in your den as a Masterpiece!

If you'd like your artwork to become a Masterpiece, click the Created Den Item button. If your Masterpiece is approved, AJHQ will send you a Jam-A-Gram to give you the good news. It could even be featured in The Daily Explorer or Jammer Central!

Then you can hang your Masterpiece on the wall of your den, post it on your Jammer Wall, recycle it to receive 1,000 Gems, give it away as a gift, or trade it!

Precious Happyflower

Precious Happyflower

Precious Happyflower

Check out these awesome frame options for your Masterpiece.

37

SPARKLING STONES

THERE ARE LOTS OF COOL THINGS TO BUY IN JAMAA— EVERYTHING FROM CLOTHES, ACCESSORIES, FURNITURE, PETS, DENS, AND MORE!

Gems

The currency in Jamaa is colorful, sparkly Gems. There are many different ways to earn Gems, and they're all fun! Playing your favorite Animal Jam games will earn you Gems. The better you are at the game, and the more you play, the more Gems you'll earn. You can also recycle any unwanted clothing, accessories, or den items for Gems. Before you do, make certain you don't want those items anymore.

FUN FACT

ONE RARE PLANT GROWS ONLY ON TOP OF DIAMOND DEPOSITS!

Diamonds

Jammers can also get some of the coolest and rarest items at the Diamond Shop! Just like Gems, Diamonds can be used to buy awesome items. The inventory at the Diamond Shop contains amazing animals, rare pets, and epic items.

ONLY IN **PLAY WILD!**

Sapphires

In Animal Jam – Play Wild! Jammers can spend Sapphires at the Sapphire Shop on awesome animals, pets, items, and more! Sapphires can also be exchanged for Gems.

Real Diamonds That Shine!

DIAMONDS ARE OLD. And when we say old, we're not kidding around. Diamonds found in kimberlite deposits were formed up to 3.3 billion years ago in the Earth's mantle. Kimberlite pipes, created by magma, connect the Earth's crust to the mantle. They carry diamonds and other rocks and minerals to the surface.

Most of the Earth's natural diamond deposits are found in Africa, although the Golconda region in India is home to one of the oldest diamond mine areas in the world. Diamonds vary in color from black to colorless. The colorless or pale blue stones are the most valued but are also the rarest. The hardness, brilliance, and sparkle of diamonds are what make them so desirable. In fact, the sparkly gem is the hardest natural substance on Earth.

The Archduke Joseph

This 76.02-carat diamond sold for nearly $21.5 million in 2012, making it one of the most expensive colorless diamonds ever sold at auction! The cushion-shaped diamond once belonged to Archduke Joseph August of Austria, for whom the gem is named.

The Centenary Diamond

A jeweler cuts a diamond to give it that brilliant sparkle it's known for. When the Centenary diamond was first mined in 1986, it weighed 599.10 carats. It took almost three years to transform it into one of the world's largest modern-cut and flawless diamonds. It's now a trim (but sparkly) 273.85 carats.

Mountain of Light

The Mountain of Light, or Koh-i-noor, diamond is mounted into the Imperial British State Crown. It dates back to 1304 and is said to be cursed! Stories say any male ruler who wears the 105.60-carat diamond will pay with his life. No wonder queens were the only British monarchs who dared to wear it!

The Hope Diamond

Throughout history, people have been willing to cheat, lie, and even kill to get their hands on diamonds. The blue Hope diamond is no different, with a past that includes theft, financial disaster, catastrophe, and death. But it sure is pretty!

The Great Star of Africa

The largest cut diamond in the world at 530.20 carats, the Cullinan I, or Star of Africa, diamond was cut from a 3,106-carat rough diamond in 1908. The fabulous diamond was mounted into the British Sovereign's Royal Sceptre. Today it's on display in the Tower of London in England.

AWESOME ADVENTURES

THE ALPHAS NEED YOUR HELP!

THE PHANTOMS HAVE RETURNED AND ARE threatening the peace of Jamaa. If you are brave, clever, and wild, you can join with the Alphas and save this world!

Help stop the Phantoms by going to the Lost Temple of Zios. Here you'll find an entrance to the Adventure Base Camp. If this is your first Adventure, make sure to visit the Training Grounds. Liza, the panda Alpha, will teach you the tips and tricks she has learned in the wild, including how to outsmart and defeat the Phantoms. You can also visit the Ocean Adventure Base Camp through Bahari Bay.

Once Liza has trained you, head to a portal to choose your Adventure. There are two modes: Normal and Hard. It might be a good idea to practice in Normal mode before tackling the Adventure in Hard mode. Some Adventures can be played with up to four Jammers. Get your best buddies together to form a dream team of Adventurers! With each Adventure you complete, your courage level will increase. The more courageous you are, the easier it will be to level up!

PECK

ALPHA TIP

ONLY IN PLAY WILD!

Adventuring with your buddies is fun, and so is playing games! From Ladybug Lane to Super Cube, there are lots of fun buddy games that are only available on Animal Jam – Play Wild!

LEARN the BASICS

Training Grounds

Learn everything you need to know to be the best Adventurer in Jamaa! Liza will give you one-on-one training to prepare you for your Adventures, including teaching you how to trap Phantoms in chomper plants. Finish this training, and you'll be unstoppable!

Proving Grounds

Join Greely, the wolf Alpha, to learn all you need to know about running and jumping in the 2-D Adventures!

Return of the Phantoms

The Phantoms have returned and Bunny Burrow is in trouble! Nasty Phantom Pipes have polluted rivers and plants that the bunnies need for a healthy home. Help Liza clean up the rivers, rescue all the bunnies, and defeat any Phantoms you encounter along the way.

The Phantom Portal

The Phantoms have opened a portal to Jamaa and have discovered how to wilt chomper plants! Find a way to revive the plants, and help Liza close the portal. Teamwork will help you work through this Adventure.

Meet Cosmo

Cosmo, the koala Alpha, needs help creating a new seed that will help defeat the Phantoms. Explore the surrounding area to find the ingredients that Cosmo needs, but watch out for Phantom Sprouters—they make more Phantoms!

The Hive

Explore the dark Phantom Hive to find the Phantom King. Make sure to bring a light! You'll meet Greely, the wolf Alpha, as you make your way through. But be on your guard—you'll need to be clever to take on the Phantom King!

#4

The Great Escape

#5

Dark sludge has started to rain down on Jamaa. Cosmo thinks it may be coming from the eerie Phantom Tower, a place that was originally built by the Alphas but is now a Phantom dungeon! To find out what the Phantoms are planning, you'll have to willingly let them capture you. Will you make it out? Only the bravest Jammers will be able to unlock the secrets of the Tower and escape!

Greely's Inferno

Jamaa's volcano is about to erupt! Can you help stop it? Head to the top to find Graham, the monkey Alpha, who will help you make your way through the volcano. You'll also discover Greely's secret lair inside. But smoking hot lava isn't all you'll have to face. With puzzles to solve and Phantoms to defeat, this Adventure promises to be a tough challenge!

#6

The Search for Greely

Greely is missing, and Graham needs your help tracking him down. Does his disappearance have anything to do with the mysterious Phantom portal discovered deep in the volcano?

#7

#8

The Forgotten Desert

Flying Jammers, this one's for you! The Phantoms destroyed five crystals that protected this area, turning it into a barren desert. Help Liza repair the crystals by collecting the missing crystal shards—but hurry! You have a limited amount of time to explore before the Phantoms return.

ALPHA TIP

GRAHAM

Adventures are filled with secret paths that can lead to hidden treasure! There's no telling how much treasure is out there, so keep your eyes peeled. Blocked passages can also be found in Adventures, but they can only be used by certain animals. If you find one of these special passages and aren't playing as the right animal, don't worry. You can play Adventures over and over again as all of your animals!

Bubble Trouble #9

Protect Jamaa's oceans in this exciting underwater Adventure! Phantoms are polluting the water and capturing the friendly dolphins that can stop them. Become your favorite ocean animal, free the dolphins, and prevent the Phantoms from destroying this precious habitat!

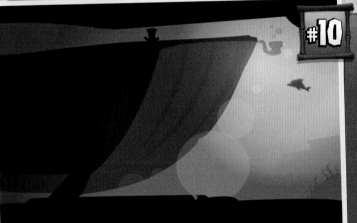

In Too Deep #10

Join forces with a squad of sharks to stop the Phantoms from polluting the ocean! The Phantoms have set up a factory that's spewing green slime into the sharks' home. Dive deep into the ocean to find the factory entrance, save the sharks, and stop the Phantoms before it's too late!

Turning the Tide

Go on a daring rescue adventure to save Tavie, the dolphin Alpha! The Phantoms have captured Tavie, and it's up to you and the brave members of the Bottlenose Brigade to defeat the Phantoms and free Tavie. The Alphas are counting on you!

#11

#12 The Hidden Falls

Graham needs your help delivering a very important message to Sir Gilbert, the tiger Alpha! A major Phantom invasion is under way, and Graham needs to warn Sir Gilbert and his troops. Jump into action and find Sir Gilbert's camp before it's too late! You'll make new friends along the way—and collect cool prizes for your efforts.

Special Adventures!

There are also a number of Adventures that come to Jamaa during specific times of the year. Jammers love earning tons of rare prizes in these seasonal Adventures!

Bitter Sweets

Lucky Clovers

Jamaaliday Rescue

Spring Festival

Special Delivery

Battle for the Beacon

#13

The Front Lines

Sir Gilbert is looking for the bravest Jammers to make their way across the battlefield and through the Phantoms' defenses. This jam-packed Adventure takes many twists and turns—are you strong enough to conquer it?

#14

The Phantom Badlands

The Phantom Badlands used to be a beautiful and peaceful place, but now the Phantoms rule this desolate wilderness. To restore it to its former glory, you must journey to a distant border to reach a hidden shrine and the ancient relic that lies within. But who could have spread all these mysterious messages throughout the land? Will someone reach the shrine before you do?

The Phantom Fortress

#15

Now that the land has been restored and saved from the Phantoms' ruin, the Phantom Fortress is stuck in place. Can you push through the Phantoms' defenses, disable the legs of the Phantom Fortress, and rescue the captured animals before the Phantoms start their march toward Jamaa?

Storming the Fortress

#16

The Phantoms have been stopped in their tracks, and it's time to take out the Phantom Fortress once and for all! Not only will you have to create a clever disguise to get in, but who knows what awaits you inside the dark Fortress?

Real-Life Adventurers

IS A LIFE OF ADVENTURE AND EXCITEMENT CALLING YOU? THROUGHOUT history, some people have been daring trailblazers, going places and doing things no one had ever done before. Learn about some of these adventurers and see what they inspire YOU to do!

Sir Ernest Henry Shackleton

His dad wanted him to be a doctor, but Irish-born Ernest Shackleton wanted a life of adventure! In 1890, at the age of 16, he joined the British Navy and eventually became a polar explorer who went on three expeditions to the Antarctic. He climbed Mount Erebus and made many valuable scientific discoveries in this vastly unexplored land. On one of Shackleton's later journeys, his ship got stuck in the ice and he and his crew had to live on floating ice for months!

Bessie Coleman

Born in 1892, Bessie Coleman dreamed of becoming a pilot. When flying schools in the United States refused her admittance, the persistent Coleman refused to take no for an answer and went to France to learn. There she became the world's first black woman to earn a pilot's license. No leisurely flights in the sky for the daring Coleman! She specialized in stunt flying, parachuting, and aerial tricks.

Neil Armstrong

On July 20, 1969, Neil Armstrong did what no other person had done before and what many believed wasn't even possible: He set foot on the moon! Armstrong knew from a young age that he wanted to be a pilot. In 1962, he joined the National Aeronautics and Space Administration's (NASA) space program and began work on the ultimate adventure: space travel. Armstrong has said that the most thrilling part of the moon mission was not his steps on the moon, but the tricky landing on the lunar surface!

And of course we can't forget ...

National Geographic Explorers Brady Barr and Tierney Thys and super scientist and veterinarian Gabby Wild! They've spent their careers protecting and studying our environment and the amazing animals that live in it. These adventurers crawl with crocodiles, explore the ocean depths, and help animals in need, then come back to Jamaa to share with us all they've learned.

ACHIEVEMENT!

over-ACHiEVERS

250
50
25
100,000

Get rewarded for your awesome accomplishments in Animal Jam!

YOU'RE PLAYING A GAME IN JAMAA WHEN ALL OF A SUDDEN YOU HEAR fireworks as a pop-up message flashes on the screen. You've earned an Achievement! These fun messages are a way of celebrating your Animal Jam accomplishments. You earn Achievements simply by exploring, playing games, or shopping.

For instance, you can earn an Achievement after you have played Best Dressed five times, or when you have purchased 25 clothing items, or for the first time you change your colors! Keep exploring and look for all the ways you can earn Achievements in Jamaa.

ALPHA TiP

COSMO

Jammers can earn plaques from AJHQ by winning contests, having their art and howls featured in Jammer Central, being featured on the Epic Dens list, and more!

Amazing Animal Achievers

SAVING LIVES? TRAVELING THE WORLD? IT'S NO PROBLEM FOR THESE AWESOME real-life animals who have achieved some truly remarkable things!

Superdog saves cats!

Most dogs like to chase or bark at cats, but not Wuffy! This kindhearted pooch has dedicated her life to rescuing cats in trouble. The first time Wuffy saved the day was when she found four sick kittens. She nursed them back to health, much to her owner's surprise! Since then, Wuffy has rescued more than 200 cats and even got a job with a local rescue group as a foster mom to cats in need.

Penguin is knighted!

It's certainly an achievement to be knighted by the Norwegian King's Guard, and it's an honor that Sir Nils Olav, the king penguin, has experienced firsthand. The Guard, who protect Norway's royal family, have been adopting king penguins as mascots because the birds' black-and-white feathers resemble the soldiers' uniforms.

Dog saves owner's life!

When Debbie Parkhurst choked on a piece of apple, her dog Tony inexplicably seemed to know exactly what to do. The golden retriever pushed Debbie to the ground and began bouncing on her chest, similar to movements used in the Heimlich maneuver. The dog's efforts dislodged the piece of apple from Debbie's windpipe and prevented her from choking!

Globe-trotting dog sees the sites!

Oscar the terrier mix has seen the Sphinx in Egypt, zip-lined in Costa Rica, ridden a camel in India, and visited the Eiffel Tower in Paris, France. He's also been on safari in Africa and had his picture taken at the Colosseum in Rome, Italy! The mild-mannered dog is a great traveler and together with his owner, Joanne Lefson, has traveled about 46,000 miles (74,030 km)! Lefson takes Oscar all over the world to prove that shelter dogs make fantastic pets.

JOURNEY BOOK

FILL YOUR JOURNEY BOOK AS YOU TRAVEL THROUGH JAMAA AND WIN PRIZES!

YOU'LL NOTICE THAT EACH land and ocean in Jamaa is home to different animals and plants. You might spot a platypus in Kimbara Outback, a rattlesnake in Coral Canyons, a hammerhead shark in Kani Cove, or a family of skunks in Sarepia Forest! When you see an animal or plant native to the land you're in, click on it. Not only will you learn awesome facts about the species, but you can add it to your Journey Book, too.

They are not all easy to find. Each land and ocean in Jamaa has its own page in the Journey Book, which is the book button on the top left of your screen. Try to match the outlines in your book to the plants and animals you see around Jamaa.

In the Field

SCIENTISTS, BIRD-WATCHERS, ARTISTS, AND even casual nature lovers keep records of animals and plants they see in the wild. If you love searching for wildlife for your Animal Jam Journey Book, you might also enjoy keeping a journal of flora and fauna you find on vacation, at a nearby park, or in your very own backyard.

All you need is a notebook and a pen or pencil. When you spot a plant, animal, or bird you want to add to your book, write down where you saw it, the date, what the weather was like, and a detailed description. Draw a picture and you'll have a great record of your real-life nature adventures.

The animals move, so sometimes you have to wait quietly until they show themselves. They might be swimming, hanging out on rocks, playing high in the treetops, or far off in the distance. Plants can blend into their surroundings so keep a lookout! You can also fill out a page of your Journey Book at the awesome Paradise Party.

The Journey Book is a fun way to learn about animals, plants, and ecosystems. Once you've found all the plants and animals in a land, you'll be rewarded with a rare and awesome prize!

Greely

ALPHA TiP

The clownfish in Crystal Reef can be hard to find. Here's a hint: These cute fish live (and hide) in sea anemones.

John James Audubon

BORN IN 1785, John James Audubon was a French-American artist, ornithologist, and naturalist who traveled the American wilderness to draw birds, animals, and plants in their natural habitats.

His life-size bird portraits and descriptions of wilderness life were first published in 1827. A huge success, Audubon's works paved the way for bird-watching to become a popular pastime in the late 1800s. It's a hobby that millions of people enjoy around the world to this day!

Named for John James Audubon, the National Audubon Society was founded in 1905. The society works to protect and conserve birds and other wildlife along with the natural ecosystems they live in.

parties

A DAY DOESN'T GO BY WHEN THERE ISN'T SOMETHING TO CELEBRATE IN JAMAA! JOIN IN AND WHOOP IT UP WILD.

LEARN ALL ABOUT THE LATEST PARTIES HAPPENING IN JAMAA BY CLICKING THE Party icon at the top of the screen. You'll see a list of the parties planned for the day and how long it will be until they start. If a party is currently taking place, there's no wait—you can join in on the fun right away!

There's another great reason to get festive—parties also allow you to buy cool party-themed items for your den, including exclusive den music and clothing.

Parties last for 30 minutes and the next one starts right after, so you'll never have to wait long to join the latest bash. You can see what's ahead by clicking the Upcoming Parties button.

If you're ready to party now, click on the Host Your Own Party button to get started! Choose a fun theme, name, and even music! Other Jammers will be able to find your party in their Party list.

PECK

ALPHA TIP

Whether you're a curious raccoon or a *baaa*shful sheep, there are a number of parties that can only be found on Animal Jam – Play Wild! that are just for you!

Fun Festivals

THROUGHOUT THE YEAR, HOLIDAYS ARE celebrated in Jamaa. Favorite among Jammers are the Jamaalidays, a series of celebrations held in the winter. Most Jammers catch the spirit of giving and give gifts to each other! Mark your calendar! Other fun celebrations include:

Friendship Festival (February)

Good buddies make Jamaa the special place that it is, so all Jammers celebrate their appreciation of friendship during this time.

Lucky Day (March)

Break out your green gear and celebrate all the lucky things in your life! If you explore Jamaa during this festival, a little extra luck might fall your way.

Freedom Day (July)

Dress up in red, white, and blue, and check out the Jamaa fireworks show!

Night of the Phantoms (October)

Jammers dress up in silly and scary costumes to trick the Phantoms and prevent them from causing mischief.

Feast of Thanks (November)

Take some time to celebrate what you're thankful for with other Jammers.

Cards shown:
NOTHING BUT LUCK!
Animal Jam r...
HORSEPLAY
HAPPY NEW YEAR!
SAY CHEESE!
SUMMER FUN!
Best Friends!

❄ JAM-A-GRAMS

JAMAA HAS ITS VERY OWN MAIL SYSTEM!

SEND MESSAGES TO YOUR BUDDIES WITH JAM-A-GRAMS, FUN POSTCARDS you can customize. Jam-A-Grams come in different themes to celebrate whatever might be happening in Jamaa. Celebrate the seasons, share your favorite animal or land in Jamaa, let buddies know you like their den or costumes, or even wish someone a happy birthday with a Jam-A-Gram.

Look for the Mail icon at the top left corner of your screen to get started. You can read messages others have sent to you and reply to them here, too. You can now choose to receive Jam-A-Grams from everyone, no one, or just buddies. Members can attach a gift to their message. Don't send anything you don't want to lose!

CHATTER MOUTHS

Hey Buddy!

Hey Buddy!

Hey Buddy!

IN ADDITION TO JAM-A-GRAMS, YOU CAN talk to other Jammers who are currently on your screen using the chat feature. In Jamaa, there are three different chat options:

Safe Chat allows you to type from a preselected dictionary of words. All new accounts start with this type of chat.

Safe Chat - Plus allows you to type words not in the preselected dictionary. This option must be turned on by your parents in the Parent Dashboard. Safe Chat - Plus is a members-only feature.

Bubble Chat lets you see other Jammers' chat and reply using prewritten messages, but you cannot type.

Chatting in the Wild

WHAT DO ANIMALS DO WHEN THEY want to send messages? In the wild, animals don't use Jam-A-Grams or chat bars. Instead, animals communicate with sight, sound, and touch, just like humans do. Some animals release chemicals called pheromones into the air to relay information. This chemical communication can be used to mark territory, attract mates, identify other animals, and find prey and food.

Kangaroos

Kangaroos will thump the ground with their powerful hind legs to warn other kangaroos of impending danger.

Fiddler Crabs

Hey, how ya doing? It's hard to miss it when these crabs wave! To attract females, male fiddler crabs wave their oversize claws in the air before tapping them on the ground.

Elephants

Elephants touch and smell each other with their trunks to form and maintain close relationships.

Cats

Cats rub faces with others or against a person's leg to transfer scents from their facial glands. It's how cats claim objects, other animals, and even people as part of their territory. When cats do this to you, they're not saying "I like you," but "You're mine!"

ALPHA TIP

GREELY

All communications in Jamaa, including Jam-A-Grams and all chat, go through the Animal Jam chat filters and are monitored by AJHQ to make sure we keep interactions fun and friendly. If you receive a Jam-A-Gram or see chat that you think breaks the Animal Jam Rules, you can use the Report button to send a message to AJHQ about that player.

EMOTeS

IF YOU'RE HAPPY AND YOU KNOW IT, USE AN EMOTE!

OR USE ONE EVEN IF YOU'RE FEELING angry, sad, surprised, or confused. Jammers can express a world of emotions by clicking on the Emotes button in their toolbar. It's an easy way to let everyone know exactly how you're feeling.

Animal Emotions

CAN ELEPHANTS GRIEVE? CAN DOGS LAUGH? STUDYING EMOTIONS IN ANIMALS IS difficult because humans are known to project their own feelings onto animals. This is called anthropomorphism. Yet research and observation have led scientists to believe that certain animals are capable of grief, love, joy, and happiness much like humans.

Elephants' Tears

When elephants are reunited with family members, what look like tears will flow down their faces. This fluid comes from elephants' temporal glands, which are between their ears and eyes. When passing the place friends or family members have died, elephants will stop for a moment to quietly stand, sometimes touching the elephants' bones.

Laughing Dogs

If you've ever seen dogs at play, you know that pooches know how to have fun! But did you know that they have their own canine laugh, too? Researchers recorded dogs playing in a park and picked up on a breathy noise that was different from normal panting. When the noise was played for other dogs, they began to play! Canine laughter must be contagious.

Sympathetic Rats

To test how helpful rats could be, one rat was placed in a cage. Another rat was allowed to move freely around it. The free rat spent a lot of time trying to open the door to help the other rat escape. At one point in the experiment the rat had a choice: to free the caged rat or snack on chocolate chips. The kind rat freed the captive first before eating—and it even shared its snack!

and ACTIONS

THAT'S NOT ALL YOU CAN DO TO EXPRESS YOURSELF!

DANCE, HOP, SLEEP, SIT, AND PLAY BY clicking on the Actions button. Dancing foxes, hopping penguins, snoozing crocodiles, and playful elephants are all common sights in Jamaa. All the animals in Jamaa are unique and their actions reflect that. Try dancing and playing when using different animals. Each animal has its own style!

THERE'S A LOT TO JUMP FOR JOY ABOUT IN JAMAA!

Hop

Play

PLEASE DON'T "PAWS" THE MUSIC!

Dance

GET READY. SET. GO! LET'S PLAY WILD IN JAMAA!

HAVING SO MUCH FUN IS EXHAUSTING. TIME FOR SOME SWEET DREAMS.

Sleep

ALPHA TIP

Sir Gilbert

There's always time to play in Jamaa! Ocean animals have a different set of Actions to choose from. They can dive, swirl, pose, play, and dance.

BUDDIES

FIND YOUR FRIENDS ANYTIME, ANYWHERE, BY PUTTING THEM ON YOUR BUDDY LIST.

JAMAA IS A BIG PLACE WITH LOTS going on. Keep track of your buddies with the Buddy List. Look for the buddies icon at the top left corner of your screen.

Jammers can have tons of buddies on their Buddy List. If your list gets full, you can turn off buddy requests by going to the icon that looks like a gear in the top right corner of your screen. You can also remove buddies from your list at any time. Be careful! Once they're removed, you'll have to find them again if you want to re-add those Jammers to your Buddy List.

MY BUDDIES

- Ajhq
- Aparri
- Bepper
- Gellyjones
- Sethyy
- Snowyclaw
- Twinkle0122
- WisteriaMoon

1000 / 1000   Search

Keep Jamaa a Friendly Place!

Here are some tips on how to make and keep friends:

- **BE KIND**
  If you get angry, don't hurt someone's feelings.

- **BE RESPECTFUL**
  Everyone is different, and that's okay!

- **DON'T GOSSIP**
  Even when the people you're talking about are not around.

- **BE SUPPORTIVE**
  True friends are happy for you when you get a cool new item or win a game. Congratulate other Jammers, too.

- **A REAL FRIEND WON'T ASK YOU TO BREAK RULES**
  Or lie, cheat, or do any other activities that can hurt you or others.

Real-Life Animal Buddies

IF TIGERS AND BUNNIES CAN BE FRIENDS IN JAMAA, WHAT'S STOPPING giraffes and goats from being friends in real life? Nothing! Check out these unusual animal buddies.

Orangutan keeps pet cat!

When Tonda the orangutan's mate died, she became very depressed. She even lost interest in her favorite hobby: painting. But when an orange tabby cat named T.K. came into her life, Tonda found something to smile about again. The orangutan, who lives in a zoo, plays with, pets, and feeds T.K. The cat inspired Tonda to start painting again. Wonder if she's done any portraits of her favorite feline friend?

Duck dotes on dog!

Don't quack up, but Cleo the Labrador retriever mix has a devoted duck pal that follows her everywhere. Sterling the duck sleeps with his head on Cleo's tummy and munches on her dog chow. The pair spend their days exploring their backyard and playing in a pond. Now isn't that just ducky!

Giraffe hangs out with goat!

Gerald the giraffe is the only one of his kind in a wildlife sanctuary in England. The zookeepers moved a friendly goat named Eddie in with him. They've been best buds ever since! Gerald licks Eddie on the head, and the goat hugs the giraffe's long neck with his legs. Don't mess with Gerald's BFF! When Eddie is bothered by the zebras who live at the sanctuary, Gerald chases them away!

ALPHA TIP

Liza

If another Jammer makes you feel uncomfortable or scared, don't respond! You should ignore them, then report and block the player, and finally, log out. Immediately tell your parents or a trusted adult. The next time you log back into Animal Jam, try choosing a different world and locking your den. If that player is on your buddy list, unbuddy them. They won't be able to bug you anymore!

perfect pets

JaMMers are the Best pet OwNers!

PETS CAN BE FOUND THROUGHOUT JAMAA OR IN Claws 'N Paws in Appondale and Flippers 'N Fins in Crystal Reef.

Once you've adopted your pet, make sure to deck it out in the latest fashions by visiting the Pet Stop! Make your new pet feel at home with den items made especially for your pets at the Pet Den Item Shop.

Some pets can be found only during certain times of the year, while others are for sale only in the Diamond Shop. Occasionally pets will be offered through Animal Jam gift cards, toys, and other merchandise. Keep exploring Jamaa until you find your perfect pet!

Anglerfish

Arctic Fox

Arctic Wolf

Armadillo

Baby Chick

Bat

Bunny

Butterfly

Cheetah

Crocodile

ALPHa TiP — GraHaM

If you adopt too many pets, you can free your pet by clicking the Pets button in your inventory and clicking on the button that looks like an open birdcage. This will set your pet free and make room for another pet.

Dolphin

Ducky

Eagle

Echidna

Elephant

Falcon

Ferret

Firefly

Fox

Frog

Gecko

Giraffe

Goat

Taking Care of Pets

The pets in Jamaa are pretty low maintenance. If you don't check in with them for a couple of days, they are just fine. But in real life it's very different: Pets are a big responsibility. They need you to take care of them every day for the rest of their lives!

If you are thinking of getting a pet, first you need to think about the right pet for your family. Does anyone have allergies? Do you have a lot of time each day to care for a pet?

Second, you need to make sure you have your parents' permission before bringing a pet into the home. It's a big responsibility, and everyone in the family should agree on whether or not they have the time, energy, money, and love for a pet. Between food, supplies, and veterinary care, pets can be expensive.

If you do get a pet, make sure to love it and take good care of it. If you do, you'll have a healthy, happy best friend who will love you back!

Pets Galore:
We love our furry friends: 47 percent of U.S. households have a dog!

Golden Armadillo

Golden Bunny

Grasshopper

Groundhog

Hamster

Hippo

Honeybee

Hummingbird

Hyena

Jellyfish

Joey

Kitty

Koala

Ladybug

Pets in Play Wild!

ONLY iN PLAY WiLD!

Need a perfect pet while playing on mobile? Play Wild! has you covered! Check out all the adorable pet options available on the app—some are even exclusive to the mobile version of Animal Jam!

Bengal Kitty
Fennec Fox
Firefly
Fuzzy Lop Bunny
Highland Pony
Honey Badger
Honeybee
Lab Puppy
Lovebug
Monarch Butterfly
Ocelot Kitty
Peacock
Pekin Rooster
Poodle Puppy
Reindeer
Rockhopper Penguin
potted Lab Puppy
Sugar Glider
Tarantula
Vampire Bat
Wild Turkey

Lemur

Lion

Llama

Lynx

Mantis

Meerkat

Monkey

Mouse

Otter

Owl

Panda

Peacock

Penguin

Phantom

Piglet

Platypus

Polar bear

Pony

65

Before You Adopt

Gabby Wild, veterinarian and wildlife conservationist, has some great advice for those who are considering adopting a pet:

Step 1: Before adopting a pet, be sure that you can care for its three basic needs: housing, food, and enrichment (behavioral training, toys, and active play).

Step 2: Meet with an adoption counselor at your local shelter to figure out which type and breed of animal is best suited for you.

Step 3: Be prepared. Most shelters provide a list of items needed to take care of your new pet. And remember: Since you and your pet are going to need time to get to know each other, consider adopting during summer vacation or over a holiday.

IN the Field with **GABBY WILD**

Puppy

Raccoon

Rare Phantom

Reindeer

Rhino

Rooster

Seahorse

Seal

Shark

Skunk

Sloth

Snake

Snow Leopard

Squirrel

Sugar Glider

Tarantula

Tiger

Turkey

Turtle

GAMER'S PARADISE

THE AWESOME GAMES IN JAMAA CAN BE PLAYED SOLO, WITH BUDDIES, OR EVEN WITH YOUR PETS!

GAMES ARE A GREAT WAY TO EARN Gems or just to have some fun! As you journey throughout Jamaa, keep your eyes open for this game controller icon to start playing. Or you can find all of the games in one place, the Sol Arcade in Jamaa Township. This arcade is chock-full of cool games to play, and you can also buy games for your den here, too.

The only games that cannot be found in Sol Arcade are ones you play with your buddies and pets. You can also click the Games icon at the top of the screen to bring up a list of every game in Jamaa, including games that you can play with your buddies. Or you can click on a buddy's name tag to invite them to a game of Bowling, Pairs, Scooped, Marbles, Shell Game, Rock Paper Scissors, Tic Tac Toe, or Four Gem. Search Jamaa to play games with some of your pets. You can choose from Disc Toss with your puppy, Ducky Dash with your pet duck, or Sssssnake with your pet snake.

For a list of all the games in Jamaa, turn to page 256.

Animals Play Wild, Too!

CREATURES OF ALL SHAPES AND SIZES LOVE TO PLAY! PLAY KEEPS their minds active and gets them moving—just like us! Check out these cool ways some animals play.

Let the games begin!

These piggies know how to bring home the bacon—and the gold medals—when they compete in the Pig Olympics in Moscow, Russia. The annual event is an Olympic-type competition, which features pig racing, pig swimming, and pigball (think soccer). Russia's specially trained pig athletes live in a complex where vets and coaches attend to their every need.

Dolphin plays with iPad!

Merlin the dolphin has an iPad app especially made for him by his trainer and dolphin researcher, Jack Kassewitz. The app shows an image of an object, like a toy duck, and after Merlin touches the screen with his nose he swims away to find it. It's an iPad scavenger hunt for aquatic animals!

He shoots! He scores!

What do fish do when they have recess from school? Play soccer! Don't believe it? Meet Albert Einstein, a calico fantail goldfish who was trained by his owner to push a ball into a goal. His owner used food pellets to train the fish. Soon Albert was pushing a weighted-down mini soccer ball into a mini goal!

ALPHA TIP

PECK

Log into Animal Jam – Play Wild! to play exclusive games like Phantom Dodger, Block Break, and more (check out the complete list on page 261)!

ONLY iN PLAY WILD!

TRADING

TRADE YOUR UNWANTED ITEMS FOR NEW ONES BY USING JAMAA'S TRADING SYSTEM!

DO YOU HAVE TOO MANY ITEMS IN your collection? Is there stuff you never wear and never want to wear again? Go ahead and trade it! It's a great, safe way to discover new items. You can add items to your Trade List so other Jammers can see what you'd like to trade. You can even check out what other Jammers are offering to trade if you're looking for cool new stuff.

If you're a little confused by the trading system, check out page 72 to find out more or click the info button at the bottom of your Trade List. You can watch a helpful video that teaches everything about trading. You'll be an expert trader before you know it!

ALPHA TIP

GREELY

Some Jammers might try to unfairly get items from others. That's why Animal Jam HQ created the trading system. If a Jammer wants to trade with you, but asks you to send them a gift through a Jam-A-Gram instead of using the trading system, don't do it. The trading system was invented to keep things fair.

Rare Items

RARE ITEMS ARE SUPERCOOL ITEMS THAT YOU CAN'T BUY ANY OLD TIME. Some are only available during certain times of the year, others can only be found on Rare Item Monday, and others are available only during a Wild Weekend sale! That's what makes them so special! The rarest items in Jamaa are marked with a gold RARE tag.

Dragon Tail

Feathered Mask

Founders' Hat

Heart Scarf

Keytar

Monster Claw

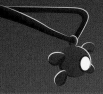

Phantom Necklace

Pirate Hook

Pirate Sword

Scary Bat Wings

Spiked Collar

Zios Mask

Trade Requested

Elvir87 wants to trade their **6** items

Precious Snowflake

6 items

for your

Do you want to trade?

TRADE ✓   ✗ CANCEL

ADD to Trade List

Q Search   SORT

TRADE SAFE!

Using the trading system is the only safe way to trade. Never agree to a trade if someone asks you in a Jam-A-Gram. Even if you agree to send your item, you can't be sure that you'll receive the other Jammer's item in return! Remember: You don't have to accept every trade. If someone sends you a trade offer that you feel is unfair or for an item you don't want, just say no!

How to Trade

#1 To choose which items you want to trade, click your animal picture. Click the Trade tab at the top, then click one of the + buttons to add items to your Trade List. These are items that you want to trade. You can even trade pets!

#2 Go to a busy area, like Coral Canyons or Jamaa Township. Stand on the edge of the crowd so that other Jammers will see you and type a message saying that you are interested in trading. You can dance or hop to get some attention!

#3 You can also go to a Trading Party, or throw one yourself! Jammers who want to trade can gather to make friends and for some swapping fun.

#4 To see what other Jammers want to trade, open their player card and click the Trade List tab. If you see an item of theirs that you like, make an offer by clicking it, then clicking the + button to add the items you want to trade.

#5 If the other Jammer likes your offer, they can accept it, and the trade is complete. Now go on and have fun trading!

I'll Scratch Your Back
If You Scratch Mine!

IN JAMAA, ANIMALS CAN TRADE A PAIR OF WINGS FOR A SOFA, BUT WHAT about in the real world? Animals don't trade objects, but sometimes they help each other out by trading services. When animals do this it's called a symbiotic, or a mutually beneficial, relationship.

Clean my teeth and eat the crumbs!

That arrangement might not sound appealing to you, but to Egyptian plovers it's a dream job. These daring birds hop right inside crocodiles' mouths to eat tiny bits of food stuck in their teeth. Why don't crocodiles eat the plovers? Because while the plovers are getting free meals, crocodiles are getting teeth cleanings that will prevent infections and keep them healthy. It's a win-win for the animals!

Help! These parasites are bugging me!

Large mammals, like hippos and water buffaloes, can be crawling with lice, ticks, and other insects. That's not fun. But what can hippos do? Find egrets that love snacking on creepy-crawlies! In addition to an all-you-can-eat bug buffet, the birds get the protection of the large animals and a free ride. In exchange, the mammals get relief from the biting and itching caused by those annoying bugs.

Let me drink your sweat and I'll protect you!

There's just something about the dew patches that rain forest caterpillars produce on their backs that are irresistible to certain ants. The ants love drinking the sweet dew so much that they will protect the caterpillar like a bodyguard. They are even known to carry the caterpillar to its nest at night for safety. Wonder if they tuck it in and read it a bedtime story, too?

JAMAA
TOWNSHIP

ANIMALS IN JAMAA GATHER TOGETHER EVERY DAY IN THE HEART OF THE LAND.

THIS BUSTLING PLACE IS WHERE JAMMERS GO TO GET the latest news, meet buddies, trade, shop, invite others to parties, see the statue of Mira, and just hang out. In the middle of Jamaa Township is Jammer Central, the place for Jammers to learn about all the cool new things going on in Jamaa.

Look for the bulletin board in Jamaa Township. That's Jammer Central! Here you'll find fun videos and cool Jammer artworks!

call this Asian city home! The world's population keeps growing and today's cities are getting bigger and bigger. Cities like Tokyo are called megacities, which have a population of 10 million or more people. Most of these megacities are located in Asia and the developing world. The U.S. has only two megacities: New York City and Los Angeles. China has the most megacities of any country in the world: four. Some people estimate that by 2030, six out of every ten people all over the world will live in a city. Jamaa Township is like some of these major cities, with shops, places to get together, and lots of exciting action!

You can read howls from other residents of Jamaa as well as submit one of your own. Lots of animals visit Jamaa Township every day, but it doesn't compare to the city that has the most people living in it: Tokyo, Japan. More than 13 million people

IN the FieLD With Dr. BraDy Barr

WILDLIFE IN THE CITY

Jamaa Township may be running wild with all different kinds of animals, but what about the town or city you call home? For people who live in rural areas, it's not so strange to have bears or coyotes as neighbors. But people living in cities are discovering wild animals in their neighborhoods, too.

The cause? Sometimes it's the lure of an easy meal. Gardens, trash cans, and bird feeders offer a smorgasbord for animals to feast on. Other times it's because the animals simply have no place else to go as humans build on the land the animals live on.

The best way to avoid having a critter as a neighbor is to not attract them in the first place. So keep garbage secured, pet food inside, and take down bird feeders in the spring.

Djemaa el Fna Square's market is open late into the night.

Market stand filled with dried fruit

STEP BACK IN TIME AND ENTER an ancient world of mysterious bazaars at the Djemaa el Fna Square, an open-air market in Marrakech, Morocco. This North African souk, or market, attracts visitors from around the world. And it's no wonder! During the day, it's an exciting shopper's paradise. If you can find your way through the labyrinth of ancient city walls, you'll discover alleys filled with shops that specialize in different items. Choose from hundreds of vendors selling jewelry, spices, carpets, and furniture, along with tourist trinkets. Listen to a storyteller spin tales of Moroccan legends

Djemaa el Fna Square

Bustling Bazaar

while you snack on freshly squeezed juice and succulent Moroccan dates.

When night falls, the market transforms into a colorful circus. Snake charmers, fortune-tellers, performing monkeys, musicians, dancers, and acrobats entertain the crowds much as they did in 1000 B.C. when Marrakech was a route for caravan traders.

If you're looking for a real-life place that is as colorful and magical as Jamaa Township, Djemaa el Fna Square might be it!

Moroccan Delicacy: A chef sells cooked snails at the bazaar.

Panda Pages: Panda poop can be made into paper!

IN THE FIELD WITH GABBY WILD

WHAT ARE BLACK AND WHITE AND CUTE ALL OVER?

Pandas, that's what! Why they have this unique coloring is another question.

Some scientists think that pandas' patches of black and white provide camouflage, while others speculate that their thick woolly coats help regulate body temperature—the black absorbs heat, while the white reflects it. Still others hypothesize

that pandas identify one another by their unique color patterns. But not because they'll want to approach someone with a familiar face; rather it's so that they can avoid one another! Pandas are solitary creatures who prefer to be alone.

STATS

GIANT PANDA

- **TYPE:** Mammal
- **DIET:** Mostly bamboo, occasionally other vegetation, fish, or small animals
- **LIFE SPAN:** 20 years
- **SIZE:** 4 to 5 feet (1.2 to 1.5 m)
- **WEIGHT:** 165 to 300 pounds (75 to 136 kg)
- **STATUS:** Vulnerable
- **WHERE THEY LIVE:** Central China

SO YOU WANT TO BE A PANDA?

THEN GET MUNCHING!

TYPICAL GIANT PANDAS spend 12 hours a day eating bamboo. Pandas have to chow down on about 28 pounds (13 kg) of the woody grasses daily because they digest only about a fifth of what they eat. Pandas' broad, flat molars are perfect for crushing the bamboo shoots, leaves, and stems that make up the majority of their diet. But all that eating leads to another call of nature. Pandas poop dozens of times a day!

Pandas live in the dense bamboo forests of central China. But pandas in the wild are in trouble. There are only about 1,800 giant pandas left. To help protect the panda, the Chinese government and conservation organizations have created sheltered areas and breeding centers for them.

Going Green: Lots of green space is a hallmark of the city of Vancouver, British Columbia, Canada.

Green Cities

COOL PLACES THAT CUT DOWN ON POLLUTION

ECO-CITIES ARE BEING CREATED around the globe as more and more people look for ways to live without harming the environment or using up natural resources.

One example of a city trying to reduce pollution and waste is Vancouver, Canada. Its admirable goal is to be the greenest city in the world by 2020! So far Vancouver has planted more than 12,500 trees, decreased total water consumption by 16 percent, added 158 miles (255 km) of bike routes to the city, increased park space, and added public charging stations for electric vehicles.

Other places face some challenging problems. Air pollution is a big problem in all of China. To make the air and water cleaner and healthier in the entire country, the government is trying to curtail the burning of coal, limit the amount of vehicle traffic, and close some factories that contribute to the smog.

But eco-cities are being built in China, too! The government is building Sino-Singapore Tianjin, a brand-new city, in the hope that one day it will be home to 350,000 residents who live in energy-efficient buildings; walk, bike, or use electric vehicles powered by renewable energy; and recycle waste and water.

Eco-Charge: Electric-vehicle charging stations are appearing in many places around the world for zero-emissions cars.

So You Want to Be a SHEEP?

Kick Back!

STATS

DOMESTIC SHEEP

- TYPE: Mammal
- DIET: Mainly grasses, hay, and oats
- LIFE SPAN: Up to 23 years
- SIZE: 4 to 6 feet (1.2 to 1.8 m) long
- WEIGHT: 44 to 441 pounds (20 to 200 kg)
- STATUS: Least concern
- WHERE THEY LIVE: Worldwide

Super Sheep: Of the more than 200 breeds of sheep, the majority have been domesticated. New Zealand has more sheep than people!

SHEEP MAY LOOK SOFT AND CUDDLY, BUT they're tough! They are also agile and quick, with excellent vision and an acute sense of smell. This allows them to perceive predators at a distance. And not only can they run fast on their hooves—they can also kick hard!

Sheep eat grass, which contains a fiber called cellulose that humans can't digest. That makes them part of the group called ruminants, because they have multiple stomachs and because they chew ... and chew ... and chew their cud. They will chew, swallow, and regurgitate their food multiple times before swallowing it for final digestion!

People in the Middle East and Central Asia domesticated these animals more than 10,000 years ago, and over the millennia these ungulates (or hooved animals) have taken up residence all over the world.

SO YOU WANT TO BE A BUNNY?

LET'S SEE YOU HOP!

OR BETTER YET, LET'S see you run. Rabbits are famous for hopping, but did you know when they really get hopping they can reach a speed of 18 miles an hour (29 km/h)? That's fast!

Rabbits are sometimes referred to as hares, but they are not the same animals. Hares are related to rabbits but generally have longer ears and hind feet than rabbits.

There are 28 rabbit species, but eastern cottontails are one of the most common. Cottontails range in color from reddish brown to gray, but all have the same adorable white "cotton ball" tail for which they are named.

Hefty Hearing: All rabbits have long ears. If you were a tasty treat to most predators, you'd want to hear if someone was sneaking up on you, too!

Are You a Bunny?

THIS IS A GREAT ANIMAL FOR JAMMERS WHO ARE ENERGETIC! LOVE TO DANCE? WATCH YOUR BUNNY'S EARS FLY WHEN DANCING IN JAMAA.

STATS

COTTONTAIL RABBIT

▸ **TYPE:** Mammal
▸ **DIET:** Grasses, herbs, buds, twigs, bark, and garden treats such as peas and lettuce
▸ **LIFE SPAN:** Less than 3 years
▸ **SIZE:** 15.5 to 18.8 inches (39.5 to 47.7 cm)
▸ **WEIGHT:** 28 to 54 ounces (800 to 1,533 g)
▸ **WHERE THEY LIVE:** Canada, South America, United States

Lovable Lifeguards: Some llamas act as guards to protect farmers' livestock from coyotes, feral dogs, and other larger predators.

Are You a Llama?

IF YOU'RE THE CURIOUS BUT GENTLE TYPE, WHO'S GOT BRAINS AND BRAWN, THEN THE LLAMA IS THE PERFECT ANIMAL FOR YOU.

... or a LLAMA?

Get Packing!

LLAMAS ARE SUPERSTURDY creatures that have lived and worked alongside people of the Andes Mountains in South America for hundreds of years. They look similar to their wild cousins, guanacos and vicunas, but all llamas have been domesticated, like cats and dogs, and were probably bred from guanacos.

As pack animals, llamas can carry a hefty 50 to 75 pounds (23 to 34 kg) of goods across the rough, rocky terrain of the Andes—sometimes up to 20 miles (32 km) in a single day!

Like cows, llamas graze on grass and regurgitate their food, saving it for later as cud, then chewing up and swallowing the wads before digestion. Llamas eat lots of different plants and require very little water, making them tough and durable, even in harsh mountainous terrain.

BUILDING the
FIRST CITIES

THERE HAVE BEEN MANY KINDS OVER HUNDREDS OF YEARS.

WE DON'T THINK OF CITIES AND FARMS as having much in common, but when early humans learned how to improve the ways they farmed and cared for animals, cities were born! In the early Neolithic period, about 9000 to 3000 B.C., people did live in villages. But they'd have to move periodically to search for better soil in which to plant their crops. This is known as a nomadic lifestyle. Imagine having to pack up your entire town and take off!

When people began to figure out better ways to cultivate the land and domesticate animals, they were able to stay put in permanent communities. Humans figured this out between 5000 and 3500 B.C. Better farming meant more food, so not everyone had to labor as farmers. Some were able to work instead as potters and weavers. Residents of the earliest urban cities were able to form governments, learn to read and write, and invent new things, which was really tough to do when they lived in seminomadic villages.

DESTINATION A.J.

SHOPPING SPOTS IN JAMAA

Jamaa Township is full of cool stores with items galore! Visit these shops to find awesome accessories for your animal and decorations for your den!

Jam Mart Furniture

Jam Mart Clothing

Sol Arcade

DIAMOND SHOP

Whip out your wallet and shop here for crystal statues, golden thrones, even royal tiaras! Whether you're looking for the coolest animals, the best accessories, or the latest and greatest dens, the Diamond Shop is filled with some of the most epic and amazing things in Jamaa.

Shop Till You Drop!

You can buy some amazing items in Jamaa, like crystal statues, golden thrones, and a royal tiara. But there are some pretty incredible things you can buy in the real world, too.

"Potty" like a billionaire with a solid-gold toilet worth $37 million.

Talk about pampered living! In 2016, U.S. pet owners spent $66 billion on their pets!

$150,000 is a lot for a cupcake that you've got to pick all the diamonds off of before you can eat it—what a pain!

This $70,000 bear has diamond and sapphire eyes, gold leaf in its fur, and a gold nose!

For $1.75 million, you can own the sQuba car and go for an underwater drive.

Sir Gilbert

ALPHA TIP

Every Monday, one super-rare item is for sale in one of the shops around Jamaa.

SO YOU WANT TO BE A PIG? PLAY IN THE MUD!

PIGS LOVE TO WALLOW in mud. But despite the rumors, these animals are actually very clean. Since they can't sweat, pigs use mud baths to cool off, rolling around to get a refreshing layer of muck on their skin. This also acts like a sunscreen, protecting them from UV rays!

Of course, it's not always mud-bath time—pigs need to eat too! In the wild, they'll eat just about anything they can find, from leaves, roots, and fruit to rodents and even small reptiles. Their special snouts, made up of cartilage and bone, act like a bulldozer as they follow their excellent sense of smell to root in the ground for food. Their tusklike canines not only aid in the excavation, they can also be used to fight!

Are You a Pig?

CUTE AND QUICK-WITTED, PIGS ARE PERFECT FOR JAMMERS WHO KNOW WHEN TO USE THEIR WITS AND WHEN TO HAVE A WALLOWING GOOD TIME!

Smart Swine: Pigs are among the smartest of all domesticated animals—even smarter than dogs!

STATS

PIG

▸ **TYPE:** Mammal
▸ **DIET:** Leaves, roots, and fruits; rodents and small reptiles
▸ **LIFE SPAN:** 12 to 27 years
▸ **SIZE:** 300 to 700 pounds (140 to 320 kg), and sometimes more
▸ **STATUS:** Least concern
▸ **WHERE THEY LIVE:** Worldwide

Growing Up Goat: Young people and young goats are both called kids. In the springtime, female goats will give birth to one or two kids.

... or a GOAT?

LIVE ON THE EDGE!

THERE ARE MANY BREEDS OF goats, from itty-bitty pygmies to 250-pound (113-kg) Anglo-Nubians. The coats of domestic goats come in a wide variety of colors, such as black, brown, tan, white, and gray. The thickness of their fur depends on where they live—a thicker layer of warmth is necessary for survival in colder climates, whereas those in warmer areas tend to have thinner, silkier coats. Both females and males boast beards and horns. During mating season, billies—male goats—will occasionally get in fights over nannies—female goats—and use their horns for battle.

STATS

DOMESTIC GOAT

- TYPE: Mammal
- DIET: Grasses and other vegetation
- LIFE SPAN: 15 to 22 years
- SIZE: Up to 3.5 feet (1.1 m) tall
- WEIGHT: 20 to 250 pounds (9 to 113 kg)
- STATUS: Least concern
- WHERE THEY LIVE: Worldwide

Market DOUBLE TAKE

See if you can spot the 10 Differences Between these two pictures.

Open-air markets in Morocco offer a variety of goods—from spices to jewelry to handmade crafts, such as painted plates, carved animal statues, and clay cooking pots.

FUN FACT

THERE'S NO NEED FOR PRICE TAGS AT A MOROCCAN SOUK, OR GRAND BAZAAR. BARGAINING IS EXPECTED, AND BUYERS AND SELLERS ARE SUPPOSED TO HAGGLE OVER THE COST OF EVERY ITEM.

Find the answers on page 262.

DUCKY DASH

JAMAA DERBY

GREAT GAMES
IN JAMAA TOWNSHIP

LOST TEMPLE OF ZIOS

A mysterious ruin in a jungle land awaits you in Jamaa—the Lost Temple of Zios. If you're ready to uncover this land's secrets, let's explore the jungle!

WHEN YOU FIRST ENTER THE DARK AND MYSTERIOUS rain forest, the sounds of insects humming, birds calling, and tree branches rustling meet your ears. But as you move in closer, a hush falls across the land. You get that funny feeling that someone, somewhere is watching you, but you're not quite sure who—or what—it is.

The truth is that potentially millions of eyes are studying your every move once you set foot in a rain forest.

Even though rain forests take up only about 6 percent of the land on Earth, they are home to about half the world's plant and animal species!

Millions of insects, reptiles, amphibians, birds, and mammals live in the rain forest. If you're not a fan of creepy-crawly creatures, this is not the place for you! The most common animals found here are invertebrates, which include insects, arachnids (yep, that means spiders and scorpions!), and worms.

Animals are not the only ones to call the rain forest home. Tribal people live in these tropical forests and survive off the land, getting food, shelter, and medicine from their surroundings.

In the rain forest of Jamaa, you'll find all kinds of creatures, including some sights you'd never see in a real rain forest—like a seal taking its pet puppy for a stroll!

DESTINATION A.J.

BRADY'S LAB

Deep in the Lost Temple of Zios, you'll find National Geographic Explorer Dr. Brady Barr's laboratory. Brady is a herpetologist— a scientist who studies amphibians and reptiles. His lab is where he hangs out and performs his experiments. But Brady's job isn't all about sitting at a desk. Check out his adventures to see close encounters with real, sharp-toothed wildlife. You can visit anytime to see all the tools he uses to learn about our planet's amazing creatures. In fact, he'll even let you explore the gear, gadgets, and gizmos he has in his lab—like his croc suit! Tag along with Brady on one of his expeditions. Help him track down giant snakes like pythons and boa constrictors!

Wandering spider

Lush Rain Forest: Lots of plant life grows in this temperate rain forest in Victoria, Australia.

DESTINATION A.J.

BRADY'S THEATER

Make sure to stop by the movie theater. Watch videos of Brady answering Jammers' questions about animals, including everything from "Why do dogs pant?" to "Do worms have eyes?" Have a burning question? Submit one of your own!

Angkor Wat is known as one of the wonders of the world.

Strangler figs grow wild over the ancient Preah Khan Temple in Angkor.

Angkor Wat

Heaven on Earth

WHAT'S ONE WAY TO MAKE SURE NO one ever forgets you? Try building the world's largest religious monument! That's what Suryavarman II did. He was king of the Khmer Empire during the first half of the 12th century when he ordered construction to begin on Angkor Wat, which means "temple city." Jamaa's Lost Temple of Zios is based on this real-life ancient place. It was built in the tropical rain forest of Cambodia in Southeast Asia over 800 years ago.

Suryavarman II wanted to re-create heaven on Earth when building Angkor Wat. So he designed it to look like Mount Meru, the legendary home of the gods in Hindu mythology. A central monument symbolizes the mythical mountain, while five towers represent its five peaks.

When you travel around the Lost Temple of Zios, you'll notice ancient statues and stone murals peeking out from the forest's foliage. These were inspired by the carvings and sculptures in Angkor Wat. It took about 5,000 artisans and 50,000

laborers more than 30 years to build and sculpt the temple complex and the many statues found there!

When it was the heart of the Khmer Empire, up to one million people lived in Angkor. Today, about two million visitors come every year to see this architectural wonder. Yet some still call this ancient city home. Villages can be found throughout Angkor where people live today. Many of them are descended from the people who built, lived in, and worked in Angkor so many years ago.

Hindu Temple: Statues and sculptures depicting scenes from Hindu religion are all over the city of Angkor.

SO YOU WANT TO BE A TIGER?

SHOW OFF YOUR STRIPES!

STATS

SIBERIAN TIGER

▸ TYPE: Mammal
▸ DIET: Deer, elk, and wild boar
▸ LIFE SPAN: 8 to 10 years in the wild
▸ SIZE: 10.8 feet (3.3 m)
▸ WEIGHT: Up to 660 pounds (300 kg)
▸ STATUS: Endangered
▸ WHERE THEY LIVE: Asia

TIGERS ARE THE WORLD'S LARGEST cats and are easily recognized by their beautiful reddish orange coat with dark stripes. Their lovely coats aren't just for show; they serve as camouflage when tigers are hunting. Tigers' stripes are like fingerprints. No two tigers have exactly the same stripes!

But tigers also have it tough. These big cats have a successful hunt only about once out of every 20 attempts. When they do make a kill, tigers have been known to eat up to 60 pounds (27 kg) of meat in one night!

There are six tiger species and they are all endangered. The cause: the hunting of tigers and the destruction of their habitat. Many conservation programs have been put in place to save these animals.

Are You a Tiger?

IF YOU WANT TO BE A TIGER, THROW BACK YOUR HEAD AND ROAR! KNOWN FOR THEIR HUNTING SKILLS AND STRENGTH, TIGERS MAKE A GREAT ANIMAL FOR JAMMERS WHO ARE PATIENT AND POWERFUL.

Solitary Cats: Tiger cubs will stay under Mom's watchful eye until they are two or three years old before going out on their own.

FUN FACT

AT AROUND SIX MONTHS OLD, CUBS TAG ALONG WITH THEIR MOTHERS ON HUNTS. BY THE AGE OF 18 MONTHS, THEY'VE LEARNED A LOT FROM THEIR MOMS AND ARE ABLE TO KILL PREY ON THEIR OWN.

IN THE FIELD WITH Dr. BRADY BARR

SPLASHING AROUND

Cats are notorious for disliking water. Have you ever tried to give one a bath? But tigers are different—they love water!

Not only are tigers good swimmers, but the big cats seem to really enjoy splashing around. They'll swim in order to hunt or to get from place to place, but tigers have been observed playing in the water, too. They've also been seen taking satisfying soaks in watering holes to cool off and relax. It's almost as if tigers have their very own hot tubs. Maybe they'd enjoy a day at the spa, too!

FLOWER POWER!

SPECIAL PLANTS SAVE THE WORLD!

THE AMAZON RAIN FOREST ALONE IS home to over 40,000 plant species. Now that's a lot of flower power! More and more, scientists are discovering that rain forest plants are very powerful. In fact, about 70 percent of plants with cancer-fighting properties come from the rain forest. And that's not all. Rain forest plants have been used to treat malaria, heart disease, diabetes, high blood pressure, and arthritis as well as many other ailments. Rain forest plants and herbs are also used in foods and cosmetics.

What makes plants found in the rain forest so special? Rain forests are crawling with insects that like to munch on the bountiful salad bar of vegetation around them. To protect themselves from all those tiny chomping jaws, plants develop chemicals to make themselves stronger and to ward off insect predators. It's these chemicals that researchers are using in medicines. New plants are always being discovered, making the rain forest a place that could potentially hold the cure for many diseases.

ALPHA TIP

Be sure to check out all the fun minibooks in the Chamber of Knowledge to learn about your favorite animals!

COSMO

Chacmool Statue: Statues depicting people sitting on the ground are thought to have been used for sacrifices or offerings to the gods.

The Temple of Kukulkan is the largest temple in Chichén Itzá.

Temple of Kukulkan

Shrine to the Gods

THOUSANDS OF JAMMERS VISIT the Lost Temple of Zios every day, but there's another temple that attracts many visitors from around the world: the Temple of Kukulkan. It's located in the ruins of the ancient Maya city, Chichén Itzá, in Mexico.

The Maya Empire included territory in southern Mexico, Guatemala, and northern Belize. At the height of their power in the sixth century A.D., the Maya excelled at mathematics, architecture, agriculture, pottery, astronomy, and calendar-making. They are also noted for having the only known written language in Mesoamerica.

The Temple of Kukulkan, also known as El Castillo, is a stair-stepped pyramid with a shrine on the top that's a testament to the importance of Maya astronomy. Its four sides face north, south, east, and west. The stairways on each face of the pyramid have 91 steps. When all four of the stairways are combined with the step on the top platform, it adds up to 365, the number of days in a year. That's not the only interesting detail. When shadows cast by the setting sun fall upon the temple during the spring and autumnal equinoxes, they resemble a snake crawling down the staircases! It's believed the temple was built to create this effect because of Quetzalcóatl, a feathered serpent who was a major deity in Maya religion. A carving of Quetzalcóatl also adorns the top of the pyramid.

Serpent God: Quetzalcóatl was a snake, and many of the statues at Kukulkan are

SO YOU WANT TO BE A SLOTH?

RELAX TO THE MAX!

Are You a Sloth?

IF YOU LOVE TO TAKE IT EASY, YOU'D FIT RIGHT IN WITH A SLOTH'S LAID-BACK LIFESTYLE!

SLOTHS ARE EXPERTS IN THE art of hanging out. In the leafy canopy of tropical trees they sleep up to 20 hours a day, waking only to forage and, once or twice a week, climb down to the ground to use the bathroom! They move slow, really slow—only up to eight feet (2.4 m) per minute. In fact, they move so slowly that algae can grow in their shaggy fur, giving it a greenish tinge. But the sluggish sloths don't seem to mind—this provides camouflage, making it more difficult for predators to spot them. But they're not always laid-back—if they do meet a hungry jaguar, they will bite, hiss, and slash with their long claws to defend themselves.

Surprising Sloths: Though sloths are sometimes mistaken for monkeys, they are actually related to armadillos and anteaters.

STATS

BROWN-THROATED THREE-TOED SLOTH

▸ TYPE: Mammal
▸ DIET: Twigs, buds, leaves, fruit
▸ LIFE SPAN: 10 years
▸ SIZE: 2 to 2.5 feet (0.6 to 0.8 m)
▸ WEIGHT: 8 to 17 pounds (4 to 8 kg)
▸ STATUS: Threatened
▸ WHERE THEY LIVE: Central and South America

Birds From the Beyond: Among some indigenous peoples, toucans are traditionally seen as a link between the worlds of the living and the spirits.

... or a TOUCAN?

PLAY CATCH!

STATS

TOCO TOUCAN

- ▶ TYPE: Bird
- ▶ DIET: Fruit; also insects, young birds, eggs, or lizards
- ▶ LIFE SPAN: Up to 20 years
- ▶ SIZE: Body, 25 inches (63.5 cm); bill, 7.5 inches (19 cm)
- ▶ WEIGHT: 20 ounces (567 g)
- ▶ STATUS: Least concern
- ▶ WHERE THEY LIVE: South American rain forests

Are You a Toucan?

IF THIS IS THE ANIMAL FOR YOU, YOU'RE PROBABLY OUTGOING AND CHATTY, AND YOU LOVE TO PLAY ALL DAY!

TOUCANS ARE FAMOUS FOR THEIR big, colorful bills. It takes several months after birth for toucans' bills to reach full size, and both males and females grow the same striking schnozzle, which is perfect for plucking fruit from the branches of trees. Though these oversize appendages look robust, they are actually made of light honeycomb bone and so don't hold up well in a fight. Fortunately, the toucans' flamboyant colors blend in well with the dappled lighting and tropical flora of the South American rain forest, hiding them in plain sight from potential predators. Not that they seem too concerned— toucans are known for the racket they make overhead, and they tend to hop from branch to branch looking for fruit or bugs. And breeding pairs toss food back and forth as part of their breeding display!

TROPICAL or TEMPERATE?

RAIN FORESTS ARE FOUND ALL OVER THE WORLD!

THE TERM "RAIN FOREST" CONJURES UP images of hot and steamy jungles teeming with exotic animals and plants. If that's true, then how can there be rain forests in Alaska? Rain forests generally have at least 100 inches (254 cm) of rainfall per year.

Tropical rain forests, like the Amazon rain forest in South America, are close to the Equator. Temperate rain forests, such as Olympic National Park in Washington, U.S.A., are located farther away from the Equator. Temperatures in tropical rain forests are warm, whereas temperate forests are cool. While hundreds of different tree species flourish in tropical rain forests, only about 10 to 20 varieties grow in a temperate rain forest. Trees in a temperate forest can be up to 1,000 years old! That's very old compared to the youngsters in the tropical rain forests, who on average are 50 to 100 years old.

Tropical and temperate rain forests may have some differences but they have one thing in common: They're both beautiful!

Keel-billed toucan

THE LARGEST AND oldest tropical rain forest in the world is the amazing Amazon rain forest. This South American forest covers an area of 2.3 million square miles (6 million sq km) and spills into Brazil, Bolivia, Peru, Ecuador, Colombia, Venezuela, Guyana, Suriname, and French Guiana. It's huge—and ancient! The Amazon rain forest is believed to be 100 million years old. It's also home to

Amazon Rain Forest

Amazing Tropical Home

a diverse range of species of insects, plants, birds, and other forms of life, many of which are not found anywhere else in the world.

While the Amazon rain forest is busy being home to all these animal, plant,

Jaguar

CHAMBER OF KNOWLEDGE

A building sits deep in the rain forest, overgrown with green vines. As you approach the stone door, a python slithers next to it, its tongue flicking in and out. As you feel your heart beat faster in your chest, the door opens as if by magic. You quickly run inside and find yourself in the mysterious Chamber of Knowledge!

On the first floor of this ancient building is a library filled with books. Learn more about the wild world around you, or continue up to the second floor to explore the artifacts and statues stored here. Make sure you walk all the way to the left of the room to find the final staircase leading to the third floor and the Mystery Emporium.

Amazing items beyond your wildest dreams are for sale in this shop. Magical objects from faraway places and statues of the Alphas are all part of the Emporium's inventory.

FUN FACT

THE AMAZON RIVER, WHICH RUNS THROUGH THE AMAZON RAIN FOREST, IS 4,000 MILES (6,437 KM) LONG—ABOUT THE DISTANCE FROM NEW YORK CITY TO ROME!

and insect species, it's also performing an important job as an air purifier. The plants in the Amazon absorb carbon dioxide in the air. Carbon dioxide is a greenhouse gas responsible for climate change. All together, the world's rain forests absorb billions of tons of carbon dioxide found in our atmosphere.

But this vitally important part of the world is in danger. During the past 40 years, close to 20 percent of the Amazon rain forest has been cut down. About 80,000 acres (32,400 ha) of tropical rain forest are destroyed daily, and experts believe the world is losing 135 plant, animal, and insect species every day as the forests fall.

Many organizations are working to protect the rain forests and the animals like jaguars, howler monkeys, tapirs, red deer, capybaras, manatees, and toucans that live here. You can lend a hand by doing something as simple as reusing and recycling paper. Every bit helps!

Howler monkey

Strawberry poison dart frog

WHO WOULD HAVE THOUGHT A TROPICAL RAIN forest has something in common with a cake? It does—layers! But unless you like munching on insects and leaves, the layers in a rain forest aren't quite as tasty. They're invaluable to the animals that live there, however.

Rain Forest
Layers

EMERGENT LAYER
There is plenty of sunshine to be found here on the treetops. Emergent trees can tower up to 200 feet (61 m) tall, almost as high as a 20-story building! Butterflies, eagles, bats, and some monkeys make their home in the emergent layer.

CANOPY LAYER
The primary layer, the canopy forms the roof of the rain forest and is a maze of leaves and branches. But the three-toed sloths, snakes, monkeys, toucans, lizards, and frogs that live here have no problem finding their way around.

UNDERSTORY LAYER
This is where things begin to get dark, because little sunshine can get through the canopy. Plants grow large here. Many insects can be found in this hot and humid layer, along with jaguars, tree frogs, leopards, owls, and bats.

FOREST FLOOR
It's damp and dark with little vegetation growing except for some moss and the giant roots of the rain forest trees. Things decay very quickly in this layer, and the floor is filled with twigs and decomposing leaves. Giant anteaters call the forest floor home and share it with other large animals like jaguars and anaconda snakes.

SO YOU WANT TO BE A MONKEY?

GO BANANAS IN JAMAA!

THE WORLD IS FILLED with monkeys! There are nearly 200 species of these cute mammals.

Monkeys are divided into two groups: Old World and New World. Old World monkeys, like baboons and colobuses, live mostly in parts of Africa and Asia, while New World monkeys live in Central and South America.

If you step into the forest and hear screeches and barks, it's most likely coming from noisy spider monkeys! These monkeys live in tropical rain forests and are perfectly built for a life in the canopy layer of the forest. Their long, lanky limbs and gripping tails let them move easily from branch to branch.

Monkey Features: New World monkeys, like this spider monkey, have large prehensile tails that they use for traveling through trees.

STATS

SPIDER MONKEY

▸ TYPE: Mammal
▸ DIET: Nuts, fruits, leaves, bird eggs, and spiders
▸ LIFE SPAN: 22 years
▸ SIZE: 14 to 26 inches (36 to 66 cm)
▸ WEIGHT: 13.2 pounds (6 kg)
▸ STATUS: Endangered
▸ WHERE THEY LIVE: Central and South America

Are You a Monkey?

KNOWN FOR THEIR PLAYFULNESS AND INTELLIGENCE, MONKEYS ARE A GREAT ANIMAL FOR JAMMERS WHO ARE FUNNY AND SMART!

103

SEEK AND FIND

LOST TEMPLE OF ZIOS Search

CAN YOU FIND THE ANIMALS IN THIS JUNGLE SCENE? LOOK CAREFULLY!

3 monkeys
1 bird's nest
3 raccoons
5 big cats
8 birds
3 pet snakes
4 torches
3 pandas
4 bunnies
2 pet turtles

Temple OF Trivia

Brady Barr's CHEMiStry Set

Sssssnake!

MiRA SAYS

FALLING PHANTOMS

GEM BALL

GREAT GAMES
IN THE LOST
TEMPLE OF ZIOS

Find the answers on page 262.

APPONDALE

GO ON safari with some of the MOST AMAZING creatures in Jamaa!

WHEN YOU STEP INTO APPONDALE, THE VISTA STRETCHES for as far as the eye can see. If you perch on the rocks next to the Claws 'N Paws tree or in the branches above it and keep looking into the distance, some of the animals that call the savanna home will show themselves!

A herd of wildebeest may come to graze on the grass, or a pair of zebras could go racing past. If you get too hot animal-watching under the bright sun, wallow in Appondale's mud pool to cool off. African animals like warthogs, elephants, and rhinos do

Great Migration: Many African animals migrate thousands of miles every year, like these in Serengeti National Park.

Tall Drinker: Giraffes don't have to bend their knees to drink at the water hole. Good thing they have long necks!

DESTINATION A.J.

CLAWS 'N PAWS

The pets in Jamaa are so adorable; you'll want to adopt them all! Claws 'N Paws is located inside Appondale's humongous tree. The tree is a baobab tree—a common sight on the savanna. These smart trees store moisture and nutrients deep in their roots that they can use during times of drought!

Pets can be found all throughut Jamaa, but in Claws 'N Paws you can find a bunch of them under one baobab roof! Snakes, kitties, puppies, turtles, frogs, ducks, butterflies, and hamsters are all available for adoption here.

this all the time in real life to beat the heat! But be warned. The mud can have an interesting effect on your animal!

Appondale is a lot like the savanna grasslands found in Africa. When an area is covered with grasses rather than large shrubs or trees, it's considered grassland. Savannas are mostly grassy areas but do have scattered trees, much like the panorama in Appondale. Savannas provide an area of transition between desert and forest.

The African savannas are huge and cover about five million square miles (12.9 million sq km) of central Africa—that's about half of the continent's surface! Large savannas are also found in Australia, South America, and India.

The recipe for making a savanna includes warm temperatures, a rainy season, and then a long period of drought.

COSMO

ALPHa TiP

Pet games are a fun way to earn Gems, but did you know that you can also play them to earn neat effects for your pet? Just collect 100 golden items with your snake, puppy, or ducky to unlock a cool effect!

Lions take a break in Serengeti National Park, Tanzania.

Flamingos flock at Lake Nakuru, Kenya, Africa.

The Serengeti

The African Safari

COME ALONG ON A FASCINATING safari through one of the oldest ecosystems on Earth. Get an up-close look at wildebeests, gazelles, lions, zebras, and hyenas as you take a tour of the Serengeti! Jamaa's Appondale is based on this real-life grassland.

Located in Tanzania, Africa, the climate, vegetation, and fauna of this 12,000-square-mile (31,080-sq-km) ecosystem has barely changed in the past million years. The local people, the Maasai, gave this seemingly boundless land its name, which means "endless plains."

During the Great Migration, over a million wildebeests, hundreds of thousands of zebras, and numerous gazelles and other animals migrate from the southeast of Serengeti toward Kenya and back to the Serengeti in search of rich grasslands and water. Visitors come from around the world to witness this spectacular sight. The instinct to migrate is so strong that nothing will stop the animals, which face predators, drought, and perilous river crossings to reach their destination. To help preserve the incredible array of wildlife found here, the Serengeti National Park and wildlife refuge was created in 1951. The park covers an area of 5,700 square miles (14,763 sq km) and is home to elephants, lions, ostriches, baboons, rhinoceroses, hippopotamuses, giraffes, cheetahs, crocodiles, leopards, and flamingos—animals you'd normally only see in a zoo!

Africa's People:
The Maasai people live in parts of the Serengeti.

SO YOU WANT TO BE A CHEETAH?

SHOW OFF YOUR SPEED!

IF YOU'RE A SPEED DEMON WITH SMOKIN' SNEAKERS, YOU'VE GOT a lot in common with cheetahs! Cheetahs are the world's fastest land mammals and can go from 0 to 60 miles an hour (97 km/h) in only three seconds! Most cars can't accelerate that fast.

These daytime hunters have a lot in their favor: exceptional eyesight, spotted coats for camouflage, and of course their scary speed! What can antelopes do? Not much. Cheetahs silently stalk their prey and get as close as possible before bolting ahead at lightning speeds. Cheetahs knocks their prey to the ground before clamping on its throat with their teeth.

Today, cheetahs are in a different race and it's not a good one. They are racing toward extinction. These cats are losing their habitat, and the numbers of the animals they prey on are declining. Botswana, Africa, is home to one of the last free-ranging cheetah populations in the world.

Are You a Cheetah?

IF YOU'RE THE TYPE OF PERSON THAT EVERYONE WANTS ON THEIR TEAM FOR A RELAY RACE, YOU'VE GOT A LOT IN COMMON WITH THE SPEEDY CHEETAH! THIS IS A GREAT ANIMAL FOR JAMMERS WHO ARE FAST AND FURIOUS!

Hunter Games:
Baby cheetahs will live with Mom for up to a year and a half, playing games with her and their siblings that teach them to become hunters.

WERE THOSE BIRDS? OR PLANES?

No, those blurs of pure speed are cheetahs, and boy, are these creatures fast! But how do cheetahs stack up against the world's fastest dog? Like cheetahs, greyhounds have small heads, large chests, and tiny waists built for sprinting at swift speeds. These dogs have been clocked as fast as 43 miles an hour (69 km/h). Cheetahs would win a race, but greyhounds would have the advantage over cheetahs that lived in a zoo their entire lives. Captive cheetahs are recorded running at speeds of 38 miles an hour (61 km/h), nowhere near the 60 miles an hour (97 km/h) of those in the wild. Researchers believe the zoo cheetahs aren't as fast as their counterparts in the wild because they've never had to run to catch food.

STATS

CHEETAH

- **TYPE:** Mammal
- **DIET:** Hares, impalas, wildebeest calves, and gazelles
- **LIFE SPAN:** 10 to 12 years
- **SIZE:** 3.5 to 4.5 feet (1.1 to 1.4 m)
- **WEIGHT:** 77 to 143 pounds (35 to 65 kg)
- **STATUS:** Vulnerable
- **WHERE THEY LIVE:** Africa and one small group in Iran

ENDANGERED
ANIMALS OF AFRICA

creatures that need our help!

WHEN ANIMALS ARE CLASSIFIED AS endangered or threatened, it means they are in danger of going extinct, or disappearing from the planet forever. They include many iconic animals such as African wild dogs, rhinoceroses, cheetahs, chimpanzees, lions, African elephants, plus several species of hyenas, gazelles, and lemurs.

The loss of habitat and prey is a reason many of these animals are endangered, but some of them face a bigger threat: poachers. Rhinoceroses are killed for their horns, elephants for their ivory tusks, and leopards for their beautiful fur coats.

There is hope. Conservation organizations are working to form antipoaching patrols, toughen laws against the illegal wildlife trade, and encourage wildlife tourism to local communities who live alongside endangered species. Once the numbers of a threatened species rise to healthy levels, they can be taken off the endangered list.

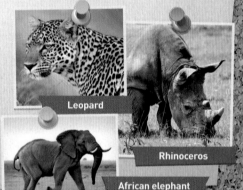

Leopard

Rhinoceros

African elephant

DESTINATION A.J.

CONSERVATION MUSEUM

We know it can be really sad to learn about all the animals that are endangered in the world. We've got some good news—Jamaa has a special place where Jammers can help these animals! The Conservation Museum in Appondale is filled with exhibits and information about endangered animals in the wild. Watch movies about big cats throughout the world and donate Gems to help conservation efforts. And you won't want to miss the Museum Shop located in the museum. It sells awesome hats (like the Panda Hat, the Bunny Hat, and the Eagle Hat) for animals to wear. Before you go, stop by the table in the middle of the room to print out fun animal info sheets!

SO YOU WANT TO BE A LION?

IT STARTS OFF AS A LOW growl. The hairs on the back of your neck stand up as the growl gets louder, turning into a ferocious roar! The roar of male lions can be heard up to five miles (8 km) away. Despite their bloodcurdling cries, lions live together in close family groups called prides. Prides consist of about a dozen females, cubs, and usually only two to three males. Male lions sometimes get a bad rap. They're labeled as lazy because the females in the pride do most of the hunting and parenting. But male lions have an important job: protecting the pride's territory. They roam areas of grasslands that can be as large as 100 square miles (259 sq km) to scare away any animals that intrude on the pride's land.

Strong Survivors: Kalahari Desert lions have learned to go without drinking water for weeks.

Let Out Your Wildest Roar!

Are You a Lion?

BE THE KING—OR QUEEN—OF THE JUNGLE WHEN YOU CHOOSE THIS AWESOME ANIMAL. THIS IS A GREAT ANIMAL FOR JAMMERS WHO ARE LOUD AND STRONG!

STATS

AFRICAN LION

▸ TYPE: Mammal
▸ DIET: Gazelles, zebras, impalas, wildebeest, and smaller animals such as birds, rodents, and fish
▸ LIFE SPAN: Up to 18 years
▸ SIZE: Head and body, 4.5 to 6.5 feet (1.4 to 2 m); tail, 26.3 to 39.5 inches (67 to 100 cm)
▸ WEIGHT: 265 to 420 pounds (120 to 191 kg)
▸ STATUS: Vulnerable
▸ WHERE THEY LIVE: Africa

SO YOU WANT TO BE AN ELEPHANT?

Raise your trunk!

ELEPHANTS ARE THE LARGEST living land animals in the world and are known for their long trunks. In addition to giving hugs, elephants' trunks are used for drinking, smelling, trumpeting, and grabbing. These useful appendages contain about 100,000 different muscles.

There are two main elephant species: African elephants and Asian elephants. In addition, smaller African forest elephants, a subspecies of African elephants, live in rain forests. African elephants are larger than their Asian cousins. Both species have tusks they use to dig for food and water and strip bark from trees. Males will use their tusks to fight each other. The tusks are made out of ivory, which has made elephants a target of poachers.

Big Eaters: Elephants can eat 300 pounds (136 kg) of food in one day.

STATS

AFRICAN ELEPHANT

▶ TYPE: Mammal
▶ DIET: Roots, grasses, fruit, and bark
▶ LIFE SPAN: Up to 70 years
▶ SIZE: Height at the shoulder, 8.2 to 13 feet (2.5 to 4 m)
▶ WEIGHT: 5,000 to 14,000 pounds (2,268 to 6,350 kg)
▶ STATUS: Vulnerable
▶ WHERE THEY LIVE: Africa

Are You an Elephant?

IF YOU LOVE TO SPEND TIME WITH YOUR FAMILY AND FRIENDS, YOU'VE GOT A LOT IN COMMON WITH AN ELEPHANT! THIS ANIMAL IS GREAT FOR JAMMERS WHO ARE FRIENDLY AND LOVING.

IT DOESN'T TAKE MUCH TO make hotheaded rhinos angry. At any sign of a threat, they'll attack.

But we can't blame these big beasts for cases of mistaken identity. They have poor eyesight and are just as likely to rush a rock as they are other animals.

There are five species of these horned mammals, whose name comes from the Greek word *rhino*, which means "nose," and *ceros*, which means "horn." If their horns break off, they can grow back. Their horns are made mostly of keratin, which can be found in your own fingernails!

... or a RHINO?
Get ready to charge!

Fierce Moms: Female rhinos aggressively protect their young from enemies while teaching them how to survive.

STATS

BLACK RHINOCEROS

- ▸ TYPE: Mammal
- ▸ DIET: Trees, bushes, leaves, and fruit
- ▸ LIFE SPAN: Up to 35 years
- ▸ SIZE: 4.5 to 6 feet (1.4 to 1.8 m)
- ▸ WEIGHT: 1,760 to 3,080 pounds (800 to 1,400 kg)
- ▸ STATUS: Endangered
- ▸ WHERE THEY LIVE: Africa

Fire: THE SavaNNa'S FrieND?

DESTINATION A.J.

PET STOP & PET DEN ITEM SHOP

Once you've adopted your perfect pet at Claws 'N Paws, make sure to visit the Pet Stop and Pet Den Item Shop. Buy your pet a fun new outfit here! Or make your new pet feel at home with a special toy or house from the Pet Den Item Shop.

The Pet Stop isn't just for pets adopted at Claws 'N Paws. Bring any of your pets here to spoil them with a special treat! You can also access the Pet Stop from the My Pets screen.

WiLDFires WORK to Keep the SavaNNa HeaLtHY!

IT SOUNDS ODD, BUT WILDFIRES ACTUALLY PLAY AN important part in the savanna's biodiversity. At the height of the dry season, fires often occur that keep the savanna healthy. The fire kills seedlings, stops grasses and trees from growing too tall, and prevents forests from spreading into the savanna. It also stops the savanna from intruding into the forest, so wildfires help maintain the borders between these two lands.

Most animals escape the fire. Smaller animals hide underground, while larger ones are able to run away. Insects, lizards, and mice are the biggest casualties of the blazes, as birds flock to feast on these critters when they try to escape the flames.

SO YOU WANT TO BE A Giraffe?

EVERYONE WILL LOOK UP TO YOU!

Lengthy Tongues: If leaves are a little too high, giraffes will put their 21-inch (53-cm)-long tongues to use!

STATS

GIRAFFE

- ▶ TYPE: Mammal
- ▶ DIET: Leaves and buds, particularly from acacia trees
- ▶ LIFE SPAN: 25 years
- ▶ SIZE: 14 to 19 feet (4 to 5.8 m)
- ▶ WEIGHT: 1,750 to 2,800 pounds (794 to 1,270 kg)
- ▶ WHERE THEY LIVE: Africa

THERE ARE PERKS TO being the tallest mammals in the world! Giraffes can reach leaves and buds in treetops that most other animals can't. Giraffes munch on hundreds of pounds of leaves a week and get most of the water they need from their plant diet. Standing up to 19 feet (5.8 m) high also allows giraffes to have an excellent field of vision, giving them an advantage when it comes to spotting a predator approaching from a distance. Lions don't have much chance of taking down a full-grown giraffe. Giraffes can run up to 35 miles an hour (56 km/h), and their lanky legs are actually quite powerful.

Are You a Giraffe?

IF YOU'RE ALWAYS LOOKING OUT FOR YOUR FRIENDS, YOU'VE GOT A LOT IN COMMON WITH THE GIRAFFE! THIS IS A GREAT ANIMAL FOR JAMMERS WHO ARE HELPFUL AND PROTECTIVE!

SO YOU WANT TO BE A CROCODILE?

Get ready to CHOMP DOWN ON SOME FUN!

IF CROCODILES LOOK LIKE LARGE prehistoric reptiles, that's because they are! Crocodiles have roamed the Earth for 200 million years. These tough predators managed to survive when dinosaurs went extinct. Scientists believe these sturdy creatures have made it for so long because they are quick learners who can adapt to changes in their environment.

Crocodiles are reptiles that belong to the same order as alligators and caimans. There are 11 species within the genus *Crocodylus.*

These amphibious lizards are the largest and heaviest reptiles on the planet! Nocturnal hunters who spend most of their time in the water, they'll come to shore from time to time to bask in the sun to help regulate their body temperature.

Are You a Crocodile?

IF THIS IS THE ANIMAL FOR YOU, YOU'RE PROBABLY THE KIND OF JAMMER WHO IS A TOUGH, QUICK-THINKER WHO KNOWS HOW TO GET BY IN ANY SITUATION.

Cunning Crocs: Nile crocodiles can kill prey as large as a water buffalo or wildebeest.

CROC ADVENTURE

I know what it's like to want to be a crocodile. In fact, I practically was one myself!

I went to East Africa to field-test my protective croc suit. This specially designed equipment looks just like a crocodile with room for me to hide inside. The goal was to get close enough to a wild croc to attach a data device to it.

Once inside the suit, I crawled up to a group of wild crocs. When I got closer, one started hissing! Would my suit protect me?

It did! I got the device on the croc's back. I proved that I can use my disguise to study wild crocodiles close up without any harm to me or them. The data logger will provide us explorers with valuable data about these animals.

To see this exciting moment, stop by my lab and watch the video!

STATS

NILE CROCODILE

▸ TYPE: Reptile
▸ DIET: Fish, turtles, birds zebras, small hippos, porcupines, other crocodiles
▸ LIFE SPAN: 45 years
▸ SIZE: 16 feet (4.9 m)
▸ WEIGHT: 500 pounds (227 kg)
▸ WHERE THEY LIVE: Sub-Saharan Africa, Egypt, Madagascar

SAVANNAS
around the world

CHECK OUT OUR PLANET'S COOL GRASSLANDS!

GRASS AS FAR AS THE EYE can see! Grasslands are vast areas of land where grass makes up most of the plant life. Technically, a grassland is mostly made up of grasses from the Poaceae family, or "true" grasses. It's one of the largest families of flowering plants, comprising around 10,000 species! This species variety gives the world's grasslands amazing diversity since it includes plants ranging from small wire grasses, bamboo, sugarcane, and even rice.

Chapada dos Veadeiros National Park, Brazil

South America
Brazil's Cerrado, which is nearly three times the size of the state of Texas, U.S.A., is a savanna full of life. Endangered species like maned wolves and giant anteaters call this grassland home.

Bandhavgarh National Park, India

Asia
The Terai-Duar savannas contain the highest concentrations of tigers and rhinos anywhere in the continent of Asia.

Arctic Ocean

NORTH AMERICA

NORTH AMERICAN PRAIRIE

EUROPE

ASIA

Pacific Ocean

Pacific Ocean

Atlantic Ocean

INDIA'S TERAI-DUAR SAVANNA

AFRICA

AUSTRALIA'S TROPICAL SAVANNA

SOUTH AMERICA

BRAZIL'S CERRADO

Indian Ocean

MAP KEY
☐ Featured Grassland
☐ Grassland

AUSTRALIA

0   2000 miles
0   3000 kilometers

ANTARCTICA

These prairies are places where the buffalo (also known as bison) roam, and the deer and the antelope play. You'll also find prairie dogs, coyotes, bobcats, wolves, and jackrabbits here.

Custer State Park,
South Dakota, U.S.A.

Mount Nameless,
Pilbara, Australia

Australia

Australia's tropical savanna is home to many animals, such as kangaroos, and the dry season can last up to five months!

121

SO YOU WANT TO BE A HYENA?

LAUGH IT UP!

THOUGH HYENAS HAVE a reputation for being scavengers, they are actually very good hunters. Like many predators, they have strong teeth and powerful jaws, and they team up with other members of their clan to hunt on the sunny savannah. Usually it's the females that lead the charge, and so not only are they first in line for dinner, they also get first dibs on baths at the local mud hole.

Hyenas are very social animals, and they have a complex system of communication, making a variety of sounds to greet one another and interact. Often females will meet at a central location within their territory in order to socialize. They make their infamous laugh-like vocalizations most frequently to tell their clan members that there is food to share—hopefully a lion won't hear the call and butt in for a seat at the feast.

Family Ties: Spotted hyenas live in large groups, called clans, which can include up to 80 members.

Are You a Hyena?

IF YOU ARE FEISTY AND DETERMINED, YOU AND A HYENA ARE A GOOD MATCH! THIS CLEVER ANIMAL IS GREAT FOR JAMMERS WHO KNOW WHAT THEY WANT AND AREN'T AFRAID TO WORK FOR IT!

STATS

SPOTTED HYENA

▸ TYPE: Mammals
▸ DIET: Hoofed mammals, including wildebeest, zebras, gazelles, impalas; also porcupines, jackals, ostrich eggs, bat-eared foxes, termites
▸ LIFE SPAN: 25 years
▸ SIZE: Head and body, 34 to 59 inches (86 to 150 cm); tail, 10 to 14 inches (25 to 36 cm)
▸ WEIGHT: 110 to 190 pounds (50 to 86 kg)
▸ STATUS: Least concern
▸ WHERE THEY LIVE: Sub-Saharan Africa

... or a LEMUR?

SOAK UP SOME SUN!

LEMURS LOVE TO SUNBATHE. At night these round-eyed, bushy-tailed animals cuddle together for protection and coziness, and by day they lounge on sun-heated rocks, arms spread wide to catch the morning's rays. Daytime is also foraging time, and troops—usually made up of 15 to 20 individuals—roam the land in search of food. In the lemur world, the females tend to be dominant. Male lemurs move around from one troop to another, but females stay with the one they were born in. That core group gets the best feeding spots, and they usually get to eat first!

STATS

RING-TAILED LEMUR

▸ TYPE: Mammal
▸ DIET: Fruit, leaves, bark, grass
▸ LIFE SPAN: 14 years
▸ SIZE: 39 inches (99 cm)
▸ WEIGHT: 22 pounds (10 kg)
▸ STATUS: Endangered
▸ WHERE THEY LIVE: Madagascar

Smelly Skirmish: Ring-tailed lemurs have "stink battles," in which they rub secretions from their scent glands into their tails and wave them at their adversaries!

On Safari

HOW MUCH DO YOU KNOW ABOUT the SPLENDID SAVANNAS OF AFRICA? QUIZ YOURSELF AND FIND OUT!

#1 Which of these spotted wild cats would you not see on an African safari?

a. leopards   **c.** servals
b. cheetahs   **d.** jaguars

#2 Giraffes sleep standing up.
True or false?

#3 African elephants use their trunks to do all of the following except _____.

a. drink water
b. smell
c. breathe while swimming
d. hold on to baby elephants to keep them close by

#4 Ostriches cannot do which of the following?

a. fly   **b.** run   **c.** kick   **d.** lay eggs

#5 All male lions have manes.
True or false?

#6 Which of these animals migrate in groups of more than a million?

a. wild dogs
b. ostriches
c. wildebeest
d. black mamba snakes

#9 Hippos are water-loving mammals that are closely related to which animals?

a. whales
b. polar bears
c. rhinos
d. house cats

#10 Which of the following apes would you find in Africa?

a. orangutans
b. chimpanzees
c. gorillas
d. both b and c

#12 What sound do spotted hyenas make?

a. meowing
b. roaring
c. whistling
d. laughing

#7 Zebras' teeth never stop growing.
True or false?

#11 Rhino horns grow from the animal's skull.
True or false?

#8 Why do Nile crocodiles bask in the sun?

a. to warm up their bodies
b. it makes them look harmless to their prey
c. to catch their breath after a swim
d. to get a suntan

THE CLAW

PEST CONTROL

PET STOP

FRUIT Slinger

DISC TOSS

GReaT GaMeS
IN APPONDALE

sarepia
FOREST

Explore the network of bridges that connect the trees and FIND OUT WHAT SURPRISES are in this forest!

AS YOU ENTER THE QUIET AND DARK SAREPIA FOREST, you notice right away the giant trees looming high above. You take a deep breath of the fresh and crisp air before heading over to a ladder. As you climb high into the treetops, keep a lookout for birds that call the forest trees home. Once you get to the top, you can do some shopping at the Flag Shop, watch a video at the Sarepia Theater, or buy some cool plants for your den's garden.

Baby Bears: Brown bear cubs stay with Mom for two and a half years.

DESTINATION A.J.

SAREPIA THEATER

Follow the bright lights to the tree house theater nestled among the tops of Sarepia's giant trees! Before catching the show, grab some popcorn or stop by the photo booth to have your picture taken in the lobby. Fireflies glow softly inside the theater itself, where you can catch National Geographic Kids movies and read cool minibooks about some of the weirdest and most fascinating animals in the world! You can also stop by the Theater Shop to stock up on stuff for movie night!

Once you're done exploring, ride the slide all the way to the forest floor—whee!

When you think of a forest, the first thing you think of is trees. There are a few different types of forests found all over the world, and one thing they have in common is trees. But trees alone do not a forest make! The forest ecosystem consists of living things like plants, animals, and microorganisms as well as soil, water, climate, and rocks.

Fox Tails: Red foxes use their tails to help them balance!

The forest ecosystem is so important that even NASA examines it! You may be surprised to learn that the National Aeronautics and Space Administration doesn't only study faraway stars and planets, but also uses its high-tech imaging equipment to map and record the changes in the forests on Earth.

ALPHA TIP

Some animals in Jamaa, like cheetahs and raccoons, come with exclusive colors that can't be chosen from the color menu!

Sir Gilbert

A biologist measures Hyperion, the tallest tree in the world.

Hikers walk through a redwood forest in California, U.S.A.

TOWERING TREE GIANTS SPAN THE redwood forests in California like leafy skyscrapers! Ancient redwood trees that thrive in the moist climate of the northern California coast can grow over 300 feet (90 m) tall and live for 2,000 years!

One by one these magnificent trees fell to loggers at the turn of the 20th century. To help protect the forests, 172-square-mile (445-sq-km) Redwood National Park was created in 1968. With its pleasant climate of mild winters and cool summers, hiking, backpacking, and camping are all popular activities. Between 1971 and 2009, more than 16 million people visited Redwood National Park.

The park is home to the tallest tree in the world, "Hyperion." It stands just over

Redwood National Park
Where Giants Live

379 feet (116 m)—three times the height of the Statue of Liberty, as measured from her heel to the top of her head. It might be tricky to go and see Hyperion in person, however. The hikers who found it and the scientists who measured it keep its location a secret to stop enthusiastic tourists from harming the tree.

Sea lions and harbor seals live off the park's coast, and gray whales can be seen as they migrate north from February to April. Roosevelt elk can be seen year-round, along with black-tailed deer, foxes, bobcats, coyotes, and chipmunks. Visitors can also see black bears!

But in Sarepia Forest, Jammers can spot crazy creatures like crocodiles, elephants, lions, and even snow leopards year round!

Heavyweights: Adult male Roosevelt elk can weigh more than 875 pounds (397 kg).

SO YOU WANT TO BE A WOLF?

THEN THROW BACK YOUR HEAD AND HOWL!

THAT'S HOW WOLVES COMMUNICATE IN THE WILD. They also talk to each other by whimpering, whining, growling, barking, yelping, and snarling.

Wolves are the largest members of the dog family. These canines are found all over the world, including Asia and the United States. Gray wolves are one of three species of wolf. The other two are eastern wolves and critically endangered red wolves. Subspecies of gray wolves, like Mexican gray wolves and arctic wolves, exist around the world.

Wolves live in groups called packs and are great at teamwork. They work together to hunt, take care of young pups, and guard their land.

STATS

GRAY WOLF

- ▸ TYPE: Mammal
- ▸ DIET: Ungulates (hooved animals like elk or bison), smaller mammals such as rodents, reptiles, and insects
- ▸ LIFE SPAN: 6 to 8 years
- ▸ SIZE: 4.5 to 6 feet (1.4 to 1.8 m) from head to tail
- ▸ WEIGHT: 50 to 110 pounds (22.7 to 50 kg)
- ▸ STATUS: Endangered
- ▸ WHERE THEY LIVE: North America, Asia, Europe

Are You a Wolf?

IF YOU'RE A TEAM PLAYER WHO DOESN'T MIND BABYSITTING YOUR LITTLE BROTHER OR SISTER ONCE IN A WHILE, YOU'LL LOVE BEING A WOLF.

Wolf Play: Wolves and our pet dogs are closely related. Wild wolves play together much like dogs do—wrestling, pouncing, and howling together.

IN THE FIELD WITH DR. BRADY BARR

Since wolf territories can range from 50 to 1,000 square miles (130 to 2,600 sq km), that means wolves sometimes have to go a long way to hunt their prey. When you're hungry, all you have to do is walk into your kitchen. Imagine having to search more than 50 square miles (130 sq km) for a snack! It's no wonder that when wolves do find food, they gobble up so much of it. In one meal wolves can eat about 20 pounds (9 kg) of meat. That would be like eating 80 hamburgers for lunch!

Comeback Pups: Gray wolves were hunted to near extinction all over the world. Now, populations are recovering.

Hero Trees

HELPING PEOPLE AND THE PLANET

FORESTS COVER MORE THAN 31 PERCENT OF the total land area of the Earth and are an invaluable resource to both humans and animals. For humans, forests provide food, shelter, wood, paper, recreation, and provide 1.6 billion people around the world with their livelihoods. Worldwide, more than 300 million people call the forest home!

If biomes could be superheroes, forests would be among the first to get a cape! Trees produce oxygen; clean the air and soil of pollution; help fight flooding, wind erosion, and noise pollution; and keep us cool. Next time you see a tree you're probably going to want to run over and give it a great big hug!

LIZA

ALPHA TIP

Something incredible will happen if a group of Jammers begin dancing next to the campfire in Sarepia Forest. The fire will grow larger and a mystical blue puff of smoke will slowly take shape. Keep dancing to see what—or who—it is!

DESTINATION A.J.

sale

TREETOP GARDENS

Plant lovers can get all their green needs, from flowers and plants to trees, at Treetop Gardens and the Topiary Shop in Sarepia Forest. Turn your den into a forest with all the flower power you can find in this treetop store! Check out the following real-life incredible gardens and gadgets.

A Garden Fit for a King

One of the most famous gardens in the world is the garden at the palace of Versailles, France. Built in the 17th century, the garden has winding paths that lead to flower beds, statues, ornamental lakes, and the Grand Canal that King Louis XIV used for gondola rides!

Food Forest

The residents of Seattle, Washington, U.S.A., are thinking big when it comes to their community garden. They're building a huge food forest, or an edible park, where city dwellers can harvest fruits and veggies for their meals for free!

Mega Greenhouses

The greenhouses of Almería, Spain, are so tightly packed together they're visible from space! These greenhouses take up about 50,000 acres (20,000 ha) and produce tons of fruits and vegetables a year.

Poison Garden

Don't make a salad from this garden! The noble residents of Alnwick Castle in England, the site of Hogwarts in the Harry Potter movie series, grow a garden that includes deadly nightshade, hemlock, and other lethal plants.

THESE PLANTS CAN KILL

SO YOU WANT TO BE A DEER?

EXPLORE JAMAA IN LEAPS AND BOUNDS!

Are You a Deer?

KNOWN FOR THEIR SPEED AND AGILITY, THE DEER IS A GREAT ANIMAL FOR JAMMERS WHO ARE QUICK AND NIMBLE!

GRACEFUL AND BEAUTIFUL deer are found around the world in forests, tundra, and grasslands. There are 47 different types of deer species including elk, caribou, and reindeer. The biggest members of the deer family are moose, which weigh in at 1,800 pounds (816 kg).

One thing most deer have in common are their antlers—worn mostly by males. The only species that doesn't have antlers are Chinese water deer. Instead, they have fanglike tusks that protrude from their mouths!

Although some species of deer are endangered, most are thriving. In the United States and Canada, deer have even become a bit of a nuisance in suburbs and cities by showing up uninvited to dine in people's gardens!

Speedsters: White-tailed deer can sprint up to 30 miles an hour (48 km/h) and leap as far as 30 feet (9 m) in a single bound!

STATS

WHITE-TAILED DEER

▸ **TYPE:** Mammal
▸ **DIET:** Grass, leaves, twigs, fruits, nuts, corn, alfalfa, lichens and other fungi
▸ **LIFE SPAN:** Up to 10 years
▸ **SIZE:** 6 to 7.8 feet (1.8 to 2.4 m)
▸ **WEIGHT:** 110 to 300 pounds (50 to 136 kg)
▸ **WHERE THEY LIVE:** North America and South America

Life Up Top: Raccoons like to build their dens high above ground. They're often found at the tops of houses or buildings.

... or a RACCOON?

PUT ON a MASK AND GET ready to PLAY!

THESE NOCTURNAL animals are most active at night. So if you're the last one to nod off at a sleepover party, you've got a lot in common with these mammals. There are seven species of raccoons, the most common being northern raccoons. Raccoons live throughout much of the world, from North and South America to Asia. In fact, these mammals can live in many different environments. They're known for being just as at home in the wilderness as they are in your backyard or in a big city.

STATS

NORTHERN RACCOON

▸ TYPE: Mammal
▸ DIET: Fruits, seeds, nuts, bird eggs, fish, frogs, crayfish, and plants
▸ LIFE SPAN: 5 years
▸ SIZE: 30 to 36 inches (76 to 91 cm) from head to tail
▸ WEIGHT: 22 to 44 pounds (10 to 20 kg)
▸ WHERE THEY LIVE: Canada, United States, and Central America

Are You a Raccoon?

LOVE TO STAY UP LATE? YOU'LL LOVE BEING A RACCOON! THIS IS A GREAT ANIMAL FOR JAMMERS WHO ARE MISCHIEVOUS NIGHT OWLS.

Forests around the WORLD

CHECK OUT OUR PLANET'S COOL FORESTS!

FORESTS COME IN ALL SIZES and types and can be found throughout the world—even in the ocean! Forests are classified by their latitude, or their distance from the Equator. But under the waves, there's another type of forest, too! All forests are home to millions of creatures big and small!

Tropical Forests

These types of forests occur near the Equator and are home to over half of the world's plant and animal species. There's no winter in a tropical forest. The average temperature is a mild 68° to 77°F (20° to 25°C), so leave the snow boots at home when visiting here!

Arctic Ocean

NORTH AMERICA

EUROPE

ASIA

Pacific Ocean

Atlantic Ocean

AFRICA

Pacific Ocean

SOUTH AMERICA

Indian Ocean

AUSTRALIA

0   2000 miles
0   3000 kilometers

MAP KEY
- Boreal Forest
- Kelp Forest
- Temperate Forest
- Tropical Forest

ANTARCTICA

Boreal Forests

Located the farthest from the Equator are boreal, or taiga, forests. The cold, harsh climate in this biome makes life for animals tough. To survive the winter, many animals hibernate or migrate to somewhere warmer. Boreal forests can be found in North America and parts of Russia and Scandinavia.

Temperate Forests

Unlike in tropical forests, the seasons do change in temperate forests located in eastern North America, parts of Russia, China, and Japan, and Western Europe. The trees lose their leaves after they turn color, from green to autumnal, in the fall. Then, trees regrow their foliage in the spring.

Kelp Forests

Kelp forests can be found in cold ocean waters and provide food and shelter for marine life. Kelp is one of the fastest growing plants in the world!

SO YOU WANT TO BE AN OWL?

SIMPLY a HOOT!

OWLS ARE NOCTURNAL BIRDS, which means that they tend to sleep during the day, and during the night they stay awake, hunting for prey. Their big eyes and wide pupils allow them to spot small rodents in the dark, though they can't move their eyes in their sockets like people can. Instead, they have special air pockets in their necks so that they can swivel their entire heads to look around—up to 270 degrees!

With their short, wide wings, owls fly quietly through the trees, then dive for the attack! Once they've caught their prey, they swallow it whole and later regurgitate pellets composed of bone, fur, and other unwanted parts.

Owls don't just hoot—they make all kinds of sounds like screeches, whistles, barks, chuckles, shrieks, coos, even a trill like a horse's whinny! Scientists believe that usually these sounds are used to signal to other owls the boundaries of their territories—and advertise their availability for potential mates.

Protecting the Nest: These birds of prey are also caring parents. Mom and Dad will defend their home and chicks from intruders at all costs.

STATS

GREAT HORNED OWL

▸ **TYPE:** Bird
▸ **DIET:** Mammals and birds
▸ **LIFE SPAN:** 5 to 15 years
▸ **SIZE:** Body, 18 to 25 inches (46 to 63 cm); wingspan, 3 to 5 feet (1 to 1.5 m)
▸ **WEIGHT:** 2 to 5.5 pounds (1 to 2.5 kg)
▸ **STATUS:** Least concern
▸ **WHERE THEY LIVE:** North and South America

Are You an Owl?
KNOWN FOR BEING WATCHFUL AND WISE, OWLS ARE GREAT ANIMALS FOR JAMMERS WHO ARE SENSIBLE AND CURIOUS!

Tons of Tail: Red pandas' tails can be 20 inches (51 cm) long—almost the length of their entire body! They wrap their bushy tails around their bodies to keep warm.

STATS

RED PANDA

- TYPE: Mammal
- DIET: Grasses, roots, fruit, acorns, berries, blossoms, bamboo leaves, small leaves of other plants, bird eggs
- LIFE SPAN: 8 years
- SIZE: Head and body, 20 to 26 inches (51 to 66 cm); tail, 12 to 20 inches (31 to 51 cm)
- WEIGHT: 12 to 20 pounds (5 to 9 kg)
- STATUS: Endangered
- WHERE THEY LIVE: Himalaya in Asia

... or a RED PANDA?

SWISH YOUR BUSHY TAIL!

SOME BIOLOGISTS THINK that red pandas belong to the bear family, while others place them in the raccoon family. Still others believe they should be in a family all their own! Whatever they are, they sure are cute! Red pandas, also nicknamed "fire foxes," don't seem to care about categories as they climb trees and munch on bamboo. Like the giant panda, red pandas have an extra wrist bone, which they use to grasp stalks of bamboo while eating the leaves. They are omnivores, though bamboo leaves are their preferred snack—up to 20,000 of them a day!

Because of their leafy diet, red pandas tend to move slowly. Combine this with their small size, and you might think they'd be easy prey. Fortunately, red pandas are cautious creatures, and they wait until the coast is clear before making their move. Plus, their bodies are built for climbing into even the thinnest branches, up and away from potential predators.

THE Tree GiANtS
Meet the Sequoia and the Redwood

TWO KINDS OF TREE TAKE THE PRIZE for being the biggest on Earth: redwoods and sequoias, which live on the West Coast of the United States.

Redwood trees are strong and sturdy. Their bark can be up to one foot (30 cm) thick and fire resistant, protecting the trees from forest fires. Some trees that have been scorched in wildfires are still alive and growing!

Giant sequoias, a species of redwood, are the largest trees in the world in terms of volume, or how much wood each one has. Redwoods grow to be the world's tallest trees, but they have a more slender trunk. But both are supertrees that provide a home for hundreds of plants and animals.

FIND OUT WHAT IT FEELS LIKE TO BE AN ant or another tiny creature by visiting Sequoia National Park. When you stand next to the ancient, towering sequoia trees you'll feel like a bug!

The park was formed in 1890 to protect the world's largest and oldest living things: giant sequoias! While Redwood National Park is home to the tallest tree, Sequoia National Park is home to the largest tree, the General Sherman Tree. Measured by how much wood the trunk alone has, which is called wood volume, the massive sequoia is esti-mated at slightly over 52,500 cubic feet (1,487 cubic m).

Neighboring Kings Canyon National Park is operated jointly with Sequoia National Park. Massive mountains and trees tower above the landscape, and seemingly bottomless can-yons and caves are carved deep into the ground. Mount Whitney, the highest peak in the United States south of Alaska, rises to 14,491 feet (4,417 m) here.

Standing Watch: Sentinel, a 700-ton (635-t) sequoia, grows right outside the Giant Forest Museum in the national park.

Visitors at the parks who observe any of the diverse wildlife that lives here—gray foxes, black bears, mule deer, bighorn sheep, kingsnakes, or California newts—can stop by the visitor center and have their find entered into the park's database of wildlife sightings. Just like a real-life Journey Book!

Fantastic Forest!

SEEK AND FIND

CAN YOU FIND THE OBJECTS IN THIS WILD SCENE? LOOK CAREFULLY!

1 raccoon
4 bears
2 squirrels
7 animals with antlers

5 wolves
1 bald eagle
2 beavers
2 bison
2 foxes

DISC TOSS

POPCORN MACHINE

SUPER SORT

WIND RIDE

THE CLAW

GREAT GAMES IN SAREPIA FOREST

Find the answers on page 262.

143

CORAL CANYONS

WALK ALONG THE ROCKY DESERT TRAILS AS YOU ADMIRE THE RED ROCK MESAS IN THIS BEAUTIFUL DESERT LAND!

EAGLES SOAR HIGH ABOVE YOU AS YOU DECIDE WHAT TO do here first. Should you dress your best for the chance to win Gems in Best Dressed? Or stop off at the Art Studio to create something amazing? In Coral Canyons, you can do that and more!

While deserts aren't barren, the idea of them as very dry is true. An area classified as a desert gets less than 10 inches (25 cm) of precipitation a year. It also has to lose more water through evaporation than it receives through rainfall.

EPIC WONDERS

Escape the heat of the Coral Canyons desert and step inside a cool cave of mystery: Epic Wonders. The entrance to this grand shop is hidden behind a waterfall that flows over the mesa.

At Epic Wonders you can buy dazzling crystal statues of the Alphas, rare birthstones, and epic den items you can't find anywhere else. The orb at the top of the stone staircase offers legendary items and accessories, which can totally transform your look!

ROYAL RIDGE

For flying Jammers, there are even more shopping opportunities in Coral Canyon. Head up high to find Royal Ridge, where you can buy special den items.

FUN FACT

DESERTS COVER MORE THAN ONE-FIFTH OF THE EARTH'S LAND!

Don't let the harsh climate fool you. Deserts are biologically rich habitats teeming with animals and plants! It's not easy, but the trick to living in the dry desert is to adapt to a life with very little water. It's something the creatures of the desert have perfected in order to survive.

Your animal may not feel the heat in Jamaa, but check out the cool animal adaptations of real-life creatures as you collect them in your Journey Book!

DESERT MYSTERIES

Fairy Circles

For a long time these mysterious circles in Africa were believed to be the footprints of gods or caused by dancing fairies. Biologists now think sand termites are the real cause!

Moving Rocks

Rocks in Death Valley, California, U.S.A., have mysteriously traveled distances of up to half a mile (0.8 km)! No one has seen them move, but they leave long tracks etched in the sand. Scientists think the cause could be found in the winter, when enough water and ice could potentially form to float the rocks.

UFOs in Roswell

In 1947, a strange object crashed into the desert outside Roswell, New Mexico, U.S.A. Although the government denies it, people to this day believe it was a flying saucer, or a UFO, complete with an alien crew!

Fennec foxes' big ears help them stay cool.

Sand dunes are formed by the wind in the Sahara.

The Sahara
Sea of Sand

IN NORTHERN AFRICA, A SEEMINGLY endless sea of sand extends over 3.3 million square miles (8.6 million sq km). This place is the Sahara, the largest hot desert in the world!

With temperatures reaching 122°F (50°C) during the hottest months, the Sahara is not a very hospitable place. Yet animals like snakes, rodents, and scorpions thrive in these extreme conditions. Gazelles, deer, baboons, hyenas, and foxes also have what it takes to tough it out in the Sahara. Lions roam the southernmost section of this desert. The lakes and pools of the Sahara are inhabited by crocodiles, frogs, and toads.

There's not a lot of Saharan vegetation, but the few grasses, herbs, shrubs, and trees that live here are heat and drought tolerant. They have to be in order to make it in this dangerous climate!

Even people manage to live here. Cities and villages are built around oases, small patches of vegetation surrounded by desert. But most people of the Sahara are in fact nomads, who live their lives moving throughout this desert landscape. The Valley of Whales is an area of the Sahara believed to have been the home of an ancient sea 37 million years ago. Today it contains an amazing collection of fossils unlike any other in the world: whales with legs! *Basilosaurus* fossils have two tiny legs that scientists believe prove modern-day whales descended from land mammals that once walked on all fours. These fossils, along with shark teeth, sea urchin spines, and the bones of giant catfish, can be seen all throughout this great valley.

Dry as Bone: Fossilized bones of ancient whales are scattered throughout parts of the Sahara, such as these in western Egypt.

COLD DESERTS

GET OUT YOUR PARKA AND EARMUFFS!

IT'S HARD TO IMAGINE, BUT COLD deserts really do exist. In fact, they are the largest deserts in the world!

While the Sahara is the world's largest hot desert, the biggest desert in the world is a polar desert. The Antarctic desert stretches over 5.5 million square miles (14.2 million sq km) around the South Pole. But where's the sand? And the heat? Remember, a desert is defined by the amount of precipitation it receives each year, not by sand or temperature. The icy floors of the Antarctic desert are made up of ice that has been there for a very long time, not from newly fallen snow or rain. Instead of being hot and dry, polar deserts are cold and dry.

The second largest polar desert is found at the North Pole and spans over the United States, Canada, Finland, Greenland, Iceland, Norway, Sweden, and Russia.

GRAHAM

ALPHA TIP

Is the stone bridge in Coral Canyons structurally sound? When three or more Jammers jump on it, it cracks. But no matter how many Jammers pile on and start hopping, the bridge has not broken—yet. I wonder what will happen when it does ...

SO YOU WANT TO BE A
POLAR BEAR?

BE BOLD IN THE COLD!

Marine Mammals: Polar bears are good swimmers, and sometimes they chase seals beneath the ice.

Are You a Polar Bear?

IF YOU'RE THE TYPE WHO ISN'T AFRAID OF A CHALLENGE, YOU'LL LOVE BEING A FEROCIOUS AND HARDY POLAR BEAR!

STATS

POLAR BEAR

- **TYPE:** Mammal
- **DIET:** Seals, walruses, seabirds, eggs, small mammals, and fish
- **LIFE SPAN:** 25 to 30 years
- **SIZE:** Up to 8 feet (2.4 m) tall
- **WEIGHT:** 330 to 1,760 pounds (150 to 798 kg)
- **STATUS:** Vulnerable
- **WHERE THEY LIVE:** Polar regions of Alaska, Canada, Greenland, Norway, and Russia

POLAR BEARS ARE FIERCE and resilient, able to survive in some of the harshest environments on Earth. To stay warm during the Arctic's cold winters, polar bears can have up to four inches (10 cm) of fat underneath their two layers of fur. They also prepare to withstand the weather by building dens, where they can wait out the worst of the storms. But maintaining body temperature isn't enough—they also need to keep themselves fed! To that end, polar bears can pick up the scent of their favorite food—ringed seals—from 20 miles (32 km) away. If polar bear moms are able to sustain a healthy weight during the winter, they will usually have one to three cubs. Polar bears are excellent mothers, protecting their offspring and teaching them to hunt so that they can survive and grow.

Desert STORMS

WATCH OUT FOR THAT DUST!

AS THE DESERT SURFACE HEATS UP, it kicks up a devil of a storm: a dust devil! When patches of ground sizzle under the desert sun, it causes the heated air near the surface to rise and spin. A spinning cylinder of hot air forms. As it travels, it picks up loose objects from the earth like dirt, leaves, and dust. Resembling tiny tornadoes, these whirlwinds of air and debris can rise hundreds of feet into the air!

Dust devils around the world have been associated with legends of evil spirits. In Africa they're thought to be demons, while in Australia parents tell their children the dust devils are spirits who will whisk them away if they are naughty! In the southwestern United States, they get their name for being, well, devilish.

DESTINATION A.J.

CANYON PATHWAYS

When leaving Coral Canyons, venture through the Canyon Pathways where you'll see cool plants and find some special pets. Be sure to play Twister while you're there!

DEN SHOP

One of the stone staircases in Coral Canyons leads to the Den Shop. Here you can get an all-new den with cool choices from a Fantasy Castle to a Sunken Ship!

SO YOU WANT TO BE A FOX?

TWITCH YOUR TAIL!

ADAPTABLE FOXES LIVE ALL OVER the world and can be found in habitats ranging from forests and grasslands to mountains and deserts.

Sly foxes are related to dogs, wolves, and coyotes. Fox species include North American gray foxes, red foxes, South American foxes, arctic foxes, bat-eared foxes, and crab-eating foxes.

When facing predators, crafty foxes know they won't win in a fight. Instead, they will try to outsmart their opponents so they can get away from them. This resourcefulness has earned foxes a reputation for intelligence.

Diverse Diet
Foxes eat mice, rabbits, fruit, eggs, birds, domesticated poultry, pet food, and even garbage.

STATS

RED FOX

▸ TYPE: Mammal
▸ DIET: Small animals, fruit, vegetables, and fish
▸ LIFE SPAN: 2 to 4 years
▸ SIZE: 30 to 55.5 inches (76 to 141 cm) from head to tail
▸ WEIGHT: 6.5 to 24 pounds (3 to 11 kg)
▸ WHERE THEY LIVE: Europe, Asia, Africa, North America, and Australia

Are You a Fox?

FOXES THINK FAST ON THEIR FEET! KNOWN FOR THEIR ADAPTABILITY AND ABILITY TO GET OUT OF A JAM, THIS IS A GREAT ANIMAL FOR SMART, SLY JAMMERS!

Water IN THE DESERT

LOOKING DEEP UNDERGROUND FOR PRECIOUS WATER

WATER IS CRUCIAL FOR survival—especially for humans! You can live for up to three days without water. After that, you'll perish! So how do people build cities in the arid desert?

Savvy desert dwellers search for groundwater below the surface of the sand in aquifers. When it rains, snows, or hails, the precipitation seeps into the ground. It can remain there for thousands of years. People in deserts often drill into the ground for this valuable resource. Aquifers are used in desert cities around the globe, including the American Southwest and the Middle East, to fulfill water needs. In the Negev, a desert in Israel, aquifers provide water for crops and even fish farming!

DESTINATION A.J.

WILD EXPLORERS TENT
Be sure to stop by the Wild Explorers Tent to watch videos that talk about the cool world around us. Visit the Explorer's desk to print out cool science projects to do at home!

A long, winding road slithers across the Gobi desertscape.

Nomadic Life: Mongolian tribes use Bactrian camels to carry goods in the Gobi.

ALTHOUGH THE GOBI DOES have areas of sand, much of it is covered in rocks! And for some—treasure!

Located in northern China and Mongolia, the Gobi takes up a total area of 500,000 square miles (1,300,000 sq km), making it the fourth largest desert in the world. The Mongolian people named it Gobi, which means "waterless place." Like all deserts, the Gobi receives very little rainfall per year. In fact, parts of this desert are completely waterless.

There's not a lot of vegetation in this dry climate, but wild camels, gazelles, and antelope roam the land. Reptiles and rodents also call the Gobi home. Very few people live in this desert and those who do are nomads who raise cattle and other livestock on the land.

Now back to that treasure! Water may be scarce, but one thing the Gobi is not lacking is fossils. In fact, a certain stretch of this desert holds a treasure trove of dinosaur and early mammal remains from the Cretaceous period, over 80 million years ago.

The Gobi
Waterless Place

Paleontologists flock to the Gobi to hunt for these rare and incredible fossil riches. The Gobi has yielded never-before-known dinosaur species, new insights into how dinosaurs lived, and dinosaur eggs complete with intact, fossilized embryos, or unhatched baby dinosaurs. Paleontologists believe they have only scratched the surface of this amazing desert land and that many more exciting finds are waiting to be discovered!

FUN FACT

A TEAM OF SEVEN PEOPLE WALKED 1,000 MILES (1,610 KM) ACROSS THE GOBI IN 51 DAYS, 11 HOURS, AND 40 MINUTES, IN TEMPERATURES AS HIGH AS 104°F (40°C)!

SO YOU WANT TO BE A FALCON?

DIP, DIVE, AND FLY!

FOR PEREGRINE FALCONS, home is where they make it. These highly adaptable birds live in a wide variety of locations, from sea level to mountainside, cold tundra to hot deserts, city to forest. Some peregrine falcons migrate in the winter from their Arctic nesting grounds all the way to South America. That's nearly 15,500 miles (24,945 km) round trip! They typically nest in shallow dips or depressions on high ledges, including those on water towers, bridges, even skyscrapers. Flying high is part of their hunting method—from that height, they have a bird's-eye view of prey down below. With incredible speed they chase or dive, then capture the prey while in flight, snatching it with their sharp talons.

Fast Falcons: Peregrine falcons can dive so fast that they can travel from the top of the Empire State Building to the ground in four seconds.

Are You a Falcon?

IF THIS IS THE ANIMAL FOR YOU, YOU'RE PROBABLY THE KIND OF JAMMER WHO IS FAST, FREE-THINKING, AND FLEXIBLE.

STATS

PEREGRINE FALCON

- ▸ TYPE: Bird
- ▸ DIET: Other birds
- ▸ LIFE SPAN: Up to 20 years
- ▸ SIZE: 40 to 43 inches (101 to 110 cm)
- ▸ WEIGHT: 19 to 57 ounces (539 to 1,616 g)
- ▸ STATUS: Least concern
- ▸ WHERE THEY LIVE: Worldwide

DO YOU FIND TRICKS MORE FUN THAN TREATS? COYOTES ARE THE PERFECT ANIMAL FOR JAMMERS WHO ARE CLEVER, HIGH-SPIRITED, AND QUICK.

Funky Feet: Coyotes have scent glands between their toes that are used to mark their territory.

... or a COYOTE?

SING ALONG!

THE CALL OF A COYOTE IS distinctive, and when the whole pack joins in, it becomes a loud and yowling chorus. These canines prefer the prairies and deserts of the western United States and Mexico, but they make a home wherever they can as human development overtakes their territories. Today, coyotes are often seen in densely populated cities, even Los Angeles, California, U.S.A.—because food is easily accessible. Coyotes will eat just about anything, including garbage when necessary.

Coyotes live in bonded family groups, and during the spring females tend to give birth to litters of between 3 and 12 pups. Both parents stick around to care for their young, making sure they are ready to hunt on their own by the following fall.

STATS

COYOTE

▸ TYPE: Mammal
▸ DIET: Rabbits, small rodents, fish, small amphibians and reptiles, insects, carrion, and even deer
▸ WEIGHT: 20 to 50 pounds (9 to 23 kg)
▸ LIFE SPAN: Up to 14 years
▸ SIZE: Head and body, 32 to 37 inches (81 to 94 cm); tail, 16 inches (41 cm)
▸ STATUS: Least concern
▸ WHERE THEY LIVE: North and Central America

LIVING IN EXTREMES

Clever animals have come up with many ways to beat the heat and find and hold on to water while living in the harsh desert. It's not easy living in a desert biome, but these animals make it work!

Gila Monster

Shun the Sun To escape the sun, some desert animals like rodents and foxes are nocturnal and come out primarily at night. Rattlesnakes and Gila monsters are crepuscular, meaning they are active only during dawn or dusk.

Fennec Fox

Self-Cooling The long ears, legs, and tails of certain desert mammals help them to expel body heat. Dark colors absorb light and trap heat; so to soak up less sun many desert animals are light colored.

Turkey Vulture

Air-Conditioning Nature's Way When desert birds like vultures urinate on their legs and feet, it's called urohydrosis, a unique way of cooling off the blood circulated through the bird's body. What a weird form of air-conditioning!

Cougar

Water Works Predators like hawks, lions, eagles, and coyotes get their moisture from the blood and water in their prey. Some animals will look for moist soil by burrowing deep underground and absorbing the water found there through their skin.

Grand Canyon

History in Stone

THE NATURAL wonders of the Grand Canyon National Park draw approximately five million visitors each year. That's a lot of people, and they're all there to see a lot of rock: 277 miles (445 km) long, about a mile (1.6 km) deep, and 18 miles (29 km) wide of it! It's no wonder Jamaa's Coral Canyons is based on this cool real-life place!

Located in Arizona, U.S.A., the Grand Canyon lies in the Colorado Plateau. Millions of years of erosion by the Colorado River created the spectacular canyon.

Desert Life

LiViNG THiNGS Beat tHe Heat!

A CARPET OF BRIGHTLY COLORED WILDFLOWERS STRETCHES in front of you, their fragrant scent filling the air. You're not in a lush meadow, but a desert. How is it possible? To survive in this dry land, desert plants have to learn how to adapt to a life with little water and temperature extremes.

Xerophytes, like cacti, are able to store water in times of drought. Other types of desert plants, phreatophytes, search out water deep underground by growing extremely long roots.

The yearly explosion of desert wildflowers happens after a seasonal rainy period. The seeds of these flowers lie dormant under the sandy soil until the rains bring them to vibrant life!

Tourists look out into the Grand Canyon from a glass-floored skywalk.

Exposed rock layers from the canyon's walls offer valuable information to geologists about the history of our planet. Some of the rocks are as old as 1.8 billion years! People have been living in the Grand Canyon for a long time, too. Human artifacts dating nearly 12,000 years old have been found here. Scientists have even discovered archaeological remains from a dozen different kinds of culture groups, including Zuni, Hopi, and Navajo.

The Hualapai tribe continues to live here on a reservation, and they manage the Skywalk, a glass floor projecting about 70 feet (21 m) over the canyon, from which brave visitors can enjoy the view.

Diverse habitats, from mountain forests to deserts, can be found in the Grand Canyon. This varied landscape means that a wide variety of wildlife calls the Grand Canyon home, including California condors, bald and golden eagles, mountain lions, bighorn sheep, coyotes, and deadly black widow spiders.

It's no wonder this amazing place is considered one of the natural wonders of the world!

So You Want to Be a COUGaR?

Silent Stalkers: Cougars don't roar. But females scream to attract males and chirp and whistle, much like birds, to signal their cubs.

Pounce Like a Pro!

COUGARS GO BY MANY names, including pumas, mountain lions, and catamounts, and can be found throughout much of South and North America. They need a lot of roaming room—only a few of these ferocious felines can comfortably share a 30-square-mile (78-sq-km) range. These cats have a poor sense of smell; they rely on their keen vision and hearing for hunting during dawn and dusk. They'll stalk their prey until the perfect moment to leap— as far as 45 feet (14 m)! If there are cubs waiting back at the den, female cougars will hide their kill under leaves and soil, then escort their litters to the spot for a meaty meal. Mothers usually have two to four cubs at a time, and they spend the first 18 months teaching their young how to hunt.

STATS

COUGAR
▸ TYPE: Mammal
▸ DIET: Deer, coyotes, porcupines, raccoons, mice, and rabbits
▸ LIFE SPAN: 9 to 12 years
▸ SIZE: Head and body, 3 to 5 feet (1 to 1.5 m); tail, 24 to 34 inches (60 to 85 cm)
▸ WEIGHT: 64 to 265 pounds (29 to 120 kg)
▸ STATUS: Least concern
▸ WHERE THEY LIVE: North and South America

Are You a Cougar?

IF YOU ARE A GREAT TEACHER WHO IS PATIENT, PROTECTIVE, AND NURTURING, THE COUGAR IS THE PERFECT ANIMAL FOR YOU!

... or a HORSE?

GALLOP to your Heart's CONTENT!

Running Free: Mustang horses roam freely on the plains of the American West.

FROM AFAR, THE SOUND OF thundering hoofbeats reaches your ears ... and then, suddenly, a herd of mustangs comes galloping into view! Mustangs are fast, graceful, and powerful tree-roaming horses. Even though mustangs roam freely, they are not technically wild horses. In fact, they are thought to be descended from Spanish Iberian horses that were first brought to the United States by Spanish explorers in the 1500s. In later years, mustangs became the main transportation of cowboys, ranchers, and pioneers. Today, they live in the western part of the United States, where they graze on open plains and travel in large herds led by a female horse (called a mare). Mustangs are slightly smaller and lighter than average horses, and are known for their speed, agility, and intelligence.

STATS

MUSTANG HORSE

- ▸ TYPE: Mammal
- ▸ DIET: Perennial grasses
- ▸ LIFE SPAN: Up to 20 years
- ▸ SIZE: 4.3 to 5 feet (1.3 to 1.5 m) at the shoulder
- ▸ WEIGHT: 750 to 1,000 pounds (340 to 454 kg)
- ▸ WHERE THEY LIVE: Western United States

159

DISCOVERING DESERTS

HOW MUCH DO YOU KNOW ABOUT COOL CANYONS AND DAZZLING DESERTS? QUIZ YOURSELF AND FIND OUT!

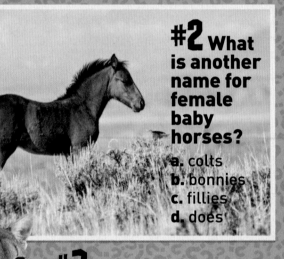

#1 When peregrine falcons spot food on the ground, they can dive as fast as 1,000 miles an hour (1,609 km/h) to snag prey.

True or false?

#2 What is another name for female baby horses?

a. colts
b. bonnies
c. fillies
d. does

#3 What cut away the rock in the Grand Canyon National Park, Arizona, U.S.A., to form the deep gorge of the canyon?

a. dynamite
b. earthquakes
c. sandstorms
d. a flowing river

#4 Cougars hunt at night using their sensitive eyes and ears, but they _____.

a. can't hear or see squirrels
b. close their eyes when they attack
c. hibernate during the winter
d. have a weak sense of smell

Find the answers on page 263.

#5 What do you call an island of plant life surrounded by desert?

a. oasis
b. isthmus
c. caravan
d. fountain of youth

#9 What color is a polar bear's skin?

a. pink
b. black
c. yellow
d. blue

#6 Fox calls sound like _____.

a. high-pitched barks
b. nothing; foxes are silent
c. piglike grunts
d. meows

#10 During the summer, the sun never sets at the North and South Poles.

True or false?

#11 It never snows in the Gobi desert in China and Mongolia.

True or false?

#7 Where can you find wild peregrine falcons?

a. Africa
b. North America
c. South America
d. both b and c

#8 Which animals might you find out at night in the desert?

a. coyotes
b. moose
c. leopards
d. alligators

CRYSTAL SANDS

THE SUN IS ALWAYS SHINING here! RELAX WHILE THE MELLOW SOUNDS OF THE OCEAN'S WAVES FILL THE AIR.

IT'S UP TO YOU IF YOU WANT TO KEEP THE LAID-BACK vibe going or if you want to play! Curl up on one of the towels on the sandy beach, have fun in the crystal clear waters, or take a ride down one of the waterslides for a splashing good time. Crystal Sands is not just a relaxation getaway, but also the gateway to Jamaa's oceans. Walk down the dock or jump in from Tierney's Aquarium to start exploring Jamaa's oceans.

Tierney's Aquarium

DESTINATION A.J.

TIERNEY'S AQUARIUM

On the sunny beaches of Crystal Sands you'll find National Geographic explorer and marine biologist Dr. Tierney Thys's aquarium. Tierney has traveled all over the world to study ocean life. She loves her work so much she wanted to share the wonders of the oceans with Jammers by setting up an aquarium in Jamaa!

Experience what it's like to be a marine biologist. Check out Tierney's tech bench with tools like underwater cameras, scooters, shark suits, and more.

Watch the fish swim by in the aquarium exhibits, or get up close and personal with marine life like rays, hermit crabs, and sea stars in the Touch Pool. Fill in the log to win cool prizes! You can also print out ocean life puzzles and pictures here. Or you can jump straight into Kani Cove right from the Aquarium.

All over the world, beaches are popular vacation destinations. They are a perfect place to relax in the sun or take part in fun activities like swimming, surfing, snorkeling, kayaking, and more! So many people enjoy beaches. But how many know exactly what a beach is?

Colorful Dives: There's so much to discover beneath the waves, as a diver (top) finds on this Dominican Republic reef. A colorful bat star and orange cup corals brighten the seafloor off Southern California, U.S.A. (above).

The area of land that lies next to an ocean, lake, or river is called a coast, or shore. Beaches are formed when waves carry crushed seashells, sand, and gravel to the shore and deposit them there. Over time, these washed-up pieces of organic matter accumulate, making the beach you spread your towel and build your sand castles on!

Beach Treasure: Sand is partly made of finely crushed seashells. But shells, rocks, and more can be found on beaches!

STRIKE A POSE! THE pale pink sands, cerulean waters, and leafy palm trees found on Anse Source d'Argent beach have made it one of the most photographed beaches in the world! This gorgeous tropical beach can be found in Seychelles, an island republic in the western Indian Ocean that's located about 1,000 miles (1,609 km) east of Kenya and 700 miles (1,127 km) northeast of Madagascar.

The Seychelles are made up of 115 islands, and though it's one of the world's smallest countries, it's home to a wide variety of marine life and lush vegetation. Jellyfish trees and the rare coco de mer plants—whose seeds weigh 66 pounds (30 kg), the largest in the plant kingdom—are among the 200 plant species on the islands. Divers can explore the turquoise waters that are home to more than 900 kinds of fish!

The three main islands of Seychelles are Praslin, La Digue, and Mahé, and all are popular tourist destinations. The Anse Source d'Argent beach is known for its coral sand surrounded by granite boulders. A reef shelters the water, protecting the beach from receiving too much wave action, making the Anse Source d'Argent surf calm, shallow, and very relaxing. There are many other

beaches in the Seychelles island chain where visitors can swim, snorkel, and surf. They all feature soft sand and crystal clear warm water, a perfect vacation combination.

Anse Source d'Argent is one of the most popular beaches in the Seychelles.

Seychelles Beaches

Tropical Paradise

Seychelles giant tortoise

DESTINATION A.J.

TIERNEY'S THEATER

Head upstairs to Tierney's Theater to relax on a beach towel while watching Tierney answer Jammers' questions about animals. If you've been wondering about ocean life, this is where you can ask her a question of your own! You can also find minibooks all about the animals of Jamaa.

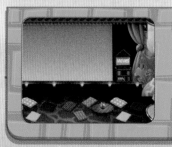

SO YOU WANT TO BE A DOLPHIN?

DOLPHINS HAVE FINS AND spend their whole lives underwater, but don't confuse them with fish! Dolphins are mammals who are warm-blooded, nurse their young with milk, and have lungs, just like humans. To breathe, dolphins must go to the surface of the water periodically to take in air through a blowhole on the top of their body. Dolphins are supersmart and social, so they make lots of noise when communicating with each other using moans, groans, squeaks, whistles, and grunts!

Dolphins can be found in every ocean in the world, and even in some rivers. Dolphins are considered to be toothed whales. There are about 40 species of dolphins, and 6 of those are commonly called whales although they are really dolphins. In fact, the orca, or killer whale, is the largest species of dolphin!

FLiP FOR FUN iN JaMaa!

Sea Smarties: Scientists use whistles and hand signals to communicate directly with intelligent and playful bottlenose dolphins.

STATS

BOTTLENOSE DOLPHIN

- ▶ TYPE: Mammal
- ▶ DIET: Fish, shrimp, and squid
- ▶ LIFE SPAN: 45 to 50 years
- ▶ SIZE: 10 to 14 feet (3 to 4.2 m)
- ▶ WEIGHT: 1,100 pounds (500 kg)
- ▶ WHERE THEY LIVE: Harbors, bays, gulfs, and estuaries in mostly temperate and tropical waters

Living Together: Penguins live together in large groups called colonies. Some species have colonies that contain millions of penguins!

STATS

LITTLE PENGUIN

▸ DIET: Fish, squid, and crustaceans
▸ LIFE SPAN: 7 years
▸ SIZE: 11.8 inches (30 cm)
▸ WEIGHT: 2.6 pounds (1.2 kg)

▸ STATUS: Least concern
▸ WHERE THEY LIVE: Coasts of New Zealand and New South Wales, Australia

... or a PENGUIN?

Put a Little Waddle in your Walk!

LITTLE PENGUINS ARE the smallest of the 18 penguin species and stand just less than a foot (30 cm) tall, while emperor penguins tower above them at a height of 45 inches (115 cm), making them the largest of the species. You may think that all penguins live in cold climates, but little penguins are found in Australia and New Zealand! These football-size birds nest in burrows on the beach, in rocky crevices, or in sand dunes. Visitors can watch colonies of little penguins waddle in from the sea and parade back to their homes each night after a day of foraging in the ocean.

Are You a Penguin?

ADORABLE AND QUICK, PENGUINS ARE PERFECT ANIMALS FOR JAMMERS WHO ARE SPEEDY AND WOULDN'T MIND LIVING WITH ALL THEIR FRIENDS!

COLORFUL BEACHES!

SANDY BEACHES are MANY DiFFereNt COLOrs!

DESTINATION A.J.

CAPTAIN MELVILLE'S JUICE HUT

All that swimming and playing on the beach can make an animal thirsty! Refresh yourself at Captain Melville's Juice Hut with your choice of delicious fruit smoothies. Look for the straw hut in Crystal Sands for this cool place to escape the sun. Try your luck at The Claw, or hop on the stage and sing a song for your fellow Jammers.

PET WASH

Stinky pet? Clean him up at the Pet Wash! Follow the rocky path up from Tierney's Aquarium to have a splashing good time with your pet.

WHEN YOU TRUDGE TOWARD THE WATER, loaded down with chairs, umbrellas, sand toys, and picnic baskets, the sand you are camping out on could be pink or even black, depending on what part of the world you are in!

Sandy beaches come in many different colors. Coral beaches are made from the eroded exoskeletons of coral and are usually white and powdery, especially in the Caribbean Sea. Some even have pink sand! The black beach berms are found on volcanic islands, including Hawaii, U.S.A. When lava flows into the ocean, it eventually cools, then explodes into thousands of tiny fragments, creating jet-black beaches.

Seeing Pink: Some of the world's pink beaches get their special hue from a type of red marine plankton called foraminifera. It mixes with white sand to look pink!

What's Underneath the Sand?

On the beach, many creatures live their lives among the grains of sand you're standing on. Some you can see, while you'd need a microscope to know the others were there!

Beach Hoppers

Tiny holes around washed-up piles of seaweed mean beach hoppers! At night, you can see these critters hopping on the sand as they search for food.

Coquina Clams

These colorful mollusks live in the top inch (2.5 cm) of sand and use the waves to move up and down the beach.

Bloodworms

These wiggly beach worms get their name from their red color. These worms can grow over 14 inches (36 cm) long!

Sand Crabs

By scooting backward, these cute crabs bury themselves in the wet sand but leave their antennae poking out.

Sand Creatures You Can't See

That bucket of sand you're using to build your sand castle? It's alive! Thousands of tiny creatures are living in it, such as water bears, or tardigrades—they're less than one millimeter long.

HELP KEEP OUR BEACHES CLEAN!

REDUCING POLLUTION AND TRASH

IMAGINE IF THE home you lived in was filled with toxic chemicals, sewage, and garbage. Unfortunately, many marine animals have to live in these conditions. Beach pollution is harmful to wildlife and humans, but you can help put a stop to it!

When you're visiting the beach, make sure to throw out your garbage in trash cans at the beach or take it home with you. Things you don't dispose of properly at home, even if you live many miles from the ocean, can still end up there. Garbage presents a choking hazard to birds and dolphins, and sea lions can get tangled up in twine, ropes, or other debris. Reducing pollution is the best way to keep our beaches healthy!

Durdle Door beach has a famous rock arch extending into the sea.

TAKING A WALK ON THE BEACHES here is more like traveling in a time machine through the Triassic, Jurassic, and Cretaceous periods! This 95-mile (153-km) stretch on the south coast of England features rocky shores, beaches, cliffs, and 185 million years of geological history. It's called Jurassic Coast, and it's brimming with fossils.

The initial fossil find was in 1811, when a 12-year-old girl named Mary Anning and her brother discovered the first complete *Ichthyosaurus* fossil. Since then, fossil hunters have flocked to the site. Mary even became one when she grew up!

Even though scientists have poured over Jurassic Coast ever since Mary's find, there are still plenty of new discoveries waiting to be found. The winter weather chips away at the fossil layers each year to reveal more hidden treasures. One of the most exciting was the skull of a giant sea monster that could have eaten a *Tyrannosaurus rex* as a snack! The ferocious 12-ton (11-t) pliosaur lived 150 million years ago.

Fossil hunting is easy on the Jurassic Coast. Fossils can be found right out in the open, lying on the ground.

Dino Coast: The coastal cliffs of Jurassic Coast are famous for fossil collecting.

Collecting them is permitted in some areas, like the beach at Charmouth. Fossils that have fallen from the overhead cliffs are considered abandoned and are up for grabs! But don't show up with a chisel and hammer to pry fossils out of the rock formations on the coast. That would be breaking the law.

SO YOU WANT TO BE A SEAL?

Make a SPLASH!

JUST EXPECT YOUR DIP IN THE ocean to be on the chilly side. Most of the 33 species of seals live their lives in cold waters. But the cold is no problem when you've got a built-in wet suit in the form of a thick layer of blubber!

Seals are broken into two groups: earless—or true—seals, and eared seals. These mammals are found all over the world, although they are more common in polar seas. Some species are found in the open ocean, while others like to live near islands, shores, or ice floes.

Are You a Seal?

SEALS ARE THE PERFECT ANIMAL FOR JAMMERS WHO ARE FRIENDLY AND LOVE TO SWIM! STAY UNDER THE SEA ALL YOU LIKE BECAUSE AS A SEAL YOU CAN HOLD YOUR BREATH BENEATH THE WAVES OF JAMAA FOR AS LONG AS YOU'D LIKE TO EXPLORE!

STATS

HARP SEAL

▸ **TYPE:** Mammal
▸ **DIET:** Arctic cod, herring, and capelin fish
▸ **LIFE SPAN:** 30 years
▸ **SIZE:** 6.2 feet (1.9 m) long
▸ **WEIGHT:** 265 to 300 pounds (120 to 136 kg)
▸ **STATUS:** Least concern
▸ **WHERE THEY LIVE:** North Atlantic and Arctic Oceans

Deep Diver: To hunt for fish and crustaceans, harp seals will dive anywhere from 300 feet (90 m) to nearly 1,000 feet (300 m).

IN THE FIELD WITH TIERNEY THYS

HARP SEALS GROW UP

The name "harp seal" comes from the large harp-shaped ring on these seals' backs. But harp seals aren't born with this marking. In fact, baby harp seals, or pups, are famous for their beautiful, pure white coats.

The pups shed their white coats after three weeks' time. When they're born, the pups don't have any blubber. But Mom's high-fat milk helps them to pack on the pounds quickly! When the pups reach about 80 pounds (36 kg), their mothers stop nursing them. They can lose about half of their body weight by the time they learn to dive into the sea to hunt for themselves.

FUN FACT

THERE'S A BEACH IN HAWAII, U.S.A., WITH GREEN SAND!

SPOT THE DIFFERENCES

BEACH DAY DOUBLE TAKE

See if you can spot the 10 differences between these two pictures.

Find the answers on page 263.

GREAT GAMES IN CRYSTAL SANDS

PET WASH

OVERFLOW!

FAST FOODIES

SMOOTHIE MACHINE

TIERNEY'S TOUCH POOL

DOUBLE UP

THE CLAW

BAHARI BAY

EVERYTHING IS PEACEFUL DOWN IN THE BAY! BOB IN THE GENTLE WAVES AS THE RELAXING MUSIC WASHES OVER YOU.

TO GET TO BAHARI BAY, TAKE A WALK TO THE DOCK IN Crystal Sands and climb down the ladder. You'll find yourself in the beautiful waters of the bay. Swim with fierce barracudas and jellyfish, watch the kelp drift in the waves, and see if you can spot elephant seals! Giant clams and sea cucumbers are abundant here. If you want to take a break from watching all the underwater life, head into Bahari Bargains. You'll find some great outfits for your ocean animals.

176

Paradise Bay:
A lone sail skims the crystal clear bay water near Nelson, New Zealand.

DESTINATION A.J.

BAHARI BARGAINS

Travel the seas in style with a little help from Bahari Bargains! This shop offers the latest in underwater fashions. Try on some seaweed hair, slip on some rainbow scales, or strap on some pufferfish spikes or a scuba helmet. To start shopping, swim through the double doors. You'll also find a special Ocean Diamond Shop that sells some of the best underwater items!

OCEAN ADVENTURE BASE CAMP

From Bahari Bay make your way to the cave with the phantom signs to find adventure! In the ocean Adventures, the Alphas need your help to foil the Phantoms' nefarious plans.

Down by the bay, where the dolphins and bears play! Bays are bodies of water that are partly enclosed by land with an outlet to the ocean. While people are fishing, crabbing, kayaking, and canoeing in bays, animals and plants are living in the waters and along the shore. The wildlife varies depending on where in the world the bay is located. Birds, fish, and insects can be found in all bay areas, while dolphins and manatees can be found splashing in some, and bears and bobcats can be seen on the shores of others!

Living on the Bay:
A woman sells fruit on a boat in Vietnam's Ha Long Bay.

Sir Gilbert

ALPHA TIP

Want a finned friend? There are lots of fun ocean pets you can adopt!

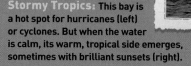

Stormy Tropics: This bay is a hot spot for hurricanes (left) or cyclones. But when the water is calm, its warm, tropical side emerges, sometimes with brilliant sunsets (right).

Bay of Bengal

One of the Seven Seas

TODAY, IF SOMEONE HAS SAILED the seven seas, it means they've traveled all the seas and oceans of the world! But to the ancient Arabs, the Seven Seas were the seven bodies of waters they sailed as part of their vital trading routes, and the Bay of Bengal was one of them.

The Bay of Bengal is the largest bay in the world and can be found in the northeastern Indian Ocean, bordered by India, Sri Lanka, Bangladesh, Myanmar, and the islands of Andaman and Nicobar. It's still part of an important trade route, and cargo from Sri Lanka, Bangladesh, and India pass through here.

Stormy weather is a part of the Bay of Bengal's climate. Monsoons are seasonal shifts in the wind's direction. These changes can bring heavy rains, thunderstorms, hail, and even tornadoes.

A cyclone is what a hurricane is called when it takes place in the Indian Ocean. These intense tropical storms happen in the Bay of Bengal during the spring and fall and bring fierce winds and flooding rains to the region.

Dreaded tsunamis also happen in this stormy bay. A tsunami is when massive waves crash from the sea onto land. These deadly waves are caused when an earthquake occurs under the sea.

Luckily, Bahari Bay is free of monsoons, cyclones, tsunamis, and other storms—it's a place where Jammers can play in gentle waves!

FUN FACT

BREEDING GROUNDS FOR ENDANGERED OLIVE RIDLEY SEA TURTLES ARE FOUND IN THE BAY OF BENGAL!

Ocean Offspring: Sea otter mothers cuddle their young and hold newborns on their chests to nurse them, until they are ready to swim and hunt for themselves.

SO YOU WANT TO BE AN Otter?

Be a Silly Swimmer!

SEA OTTERS ARE FAMOUS for their playful antics both in and out of the water. They are excellent swimmers, with their webbed feet, ability to close their nostrils and ears, and water-repellent fur that keeps them warm and dry.

Otters rest and hang out with friends and family in groups called rafts. Together they float upon the water's surface, sometimes in forests of kelp, or giant seaweed. At times they'll even hold hands! Being entangled keeps them from moving too much in the roiling sea. While bobbing on their backs, sometimes sea otters nap, while at other times they use rocks to open mussels or other shellfish by placing a rock on their chests and smashing the shellfish against it until it breaks open, then eating the tasty meat inside.

Are You an Otter?

LOVE TO SWIM AND PLAY? THIS ANIMAL IS GREAT FOR JAMMERS WHO ARE LIVELY AND FUN-LOVING.

Perfectly Pink: Flamingos' main food source are brine shrimp, which eat algae that contains beta-carotene. This chemical is also found in spinach and carrots, and it is what turns flamingos' feathers pink!

STATS

GREATER FLAMINGO

- TYPE: Bird
- DIET: Bacteria, worms, crustaceans, insects, and small fish
- LIFE SPAN: 16.3 years
- SIZE: 36 to 50 inches (91 to 127 cm)
- WEIGHT: 9 pounds (4 kg)
- STATUS: Least concern
- WHERE THEY LIVE: South Europe, South Asia, Africa, and the Middle East

SHOW YOUR TRUE COLORS IN JAMAA!

WHEN FLAMINGOS ARE born, they are gray or white, with a straight bill and soft, downy feathers. Parents are able to recognize their chick by its voice, and they feed it a special fluid to help it grow. And boy, do these baby birds grow! Within the first couple of years after birth, their feathers turn a bright, flamboyant pink, and their black-tipped bill curves into a scoop-shaped beak. Standing high above the surface of the water on stilt-like legs, they weave and bob their S-shaped necks as they look for a tasty snack. Thanks to their webbed feet, they can "run" on water, which they do to gain speed before lifting off in flight.

... or a FLAMINGO?

Are You a Flamingo?

FOR JAMMERS WHO LIKE TO STAND OUT, THE FLAMINGO IS THE ANIMAL FOR YOU! BRIGHT AND BOLD, YOU LOVE TO WEAR LOTS OF FLAIR!

DOWN BY THE GULF!

DOWN BY THE BAY—OR DOWN BY THE GULF? LIKE A BAY, A GULF IS also partly surrounded by land. Usually gulfs are larger than bays, but not always. The Bay of Bengal occupies an area of 839,000 square miles (2,173,000 sq km), while the Gulf of Mexico is only 600,000 square miles (1,550,000 sq km).

There's no one clear defining factor to tell the two apart, but here's one tidbit of information you can tuck away for a trivia game: Both gulfs and bays have outlets to the ocean, but the outlets in gulfs are normally narrower than the wider bay ones. Whatever you call them, they're fun places to visit!

Bay-loving harbor **seals** bask in the sun.

San Francisco's Golden Gate Bridge

MORE THAN SEVEN MILLION people live in the cities and towns around the San Francisco Bay in California, U.S.A. The San Francisco Bay connects to the Pacific Ocean through the Golden Gate strait. You may have heard of the famous bridge that spans this strait, the Golden Gate Bridge! The bay itself is 60 miles (97 km) long and up to 12 miles (19 km) wide and contains beautiful harbors, many islands, and a multitude of wildlife species, including endangered ones.

Watch 18 species of whales in the bay and estuary, including blue whales and gray whales. Dolphins and porpoises play and hunt in the bay. Sharks, like the colorful leopard shark, live here, too.

The San Francisco Bay is also used as a nursery for all types of animals. For broadnose sevengill sharks, it's one of two places they come to have their pups. Hundreds of species of birds nest here, including endangered California clapper rails. Harbor seals come ashore to birth and raise their pups.

Common mammals like squirrels, rabbits, raccoons, and foxes live here, but mountain lions, bobcats, badgers, and elk also roam the Bay Area. Marine mammals like sea otters and elephant seals splash in the bay waters. Frogs, salamanders, newts, turtles, snakes, spiders, and butterflies are also plentiful!

Being so close to an urban landscape has drawbacks, the biggest being pollution. There are a number of wildlife organizations working to protect this amazing habitat that's so full of life.

FUN FACT

THE SAN FRANCISCO BAY'S ALCATRAZ ISLAND, HOME OF THE FORMER MAXIMUM SECURITY PRISON, WAS ALSO THE LOCATION OF THE FIRST LIGHTHOUSE ON THE WEST COAST OF THE UNITED STATES.

FUN FACT

LONESOME GEORGE THE GALÁPAGOS TORTOISE WAS THE LAST OF HIS SUBSPECIES. SCIENTISTS ESTIMATE HE WAS ABOUT 100 YEARS OLD.

SEEK AND FIND

A DAY BY THE BAY

CAN YOU FIND THE
OBJECTS IN THIS
GALÁPAGOS SCENE?
LOOK CAREFULLY!

3	iguanas	1	Galápagos tortoise
6	crabs	4	blue-footed boobies
1	penguin	4	flamingos
3	snorkelers	1	pair of sunglasses
3	cactus trees		
3	sea lions		

GREAT GAMES
IN BAHARI BAY

Find the answers on page 263.

CRYSTAL REEF

AN UNDERWATER RAINBOW OF VIVID COLOR GREETS YOU AS YOU SPLASH INTO CRYSTAL REEF!

T HIS VIBRANT PLACE IS FILLED WITH PLANT AND ANIMAL life. Dive into the warm, crystal clear waters and get ready to explore! As you swim through the colorful coral and tube sponges, keep your eyes peeled for stingrays and even humpback whales!

While you're there, don't forget to visit Flippers 'N Fins to find the perfect aquatic pet.

Swimming With Coral: Divers take in the undersea sights off the Andaman Islands in the Indian Ocean.

Toxic Tail: Stingrays have poisonous barbs on their tails that are only used in self-defense.

Seahorses, turtles, jellies, and anglerfish are waiting to tag along on all of your ocean adventures and make loyal companions. To visit Crystal Reef, you'll need an ocean animal.

Like rain forests, coral reefs are home to a large variety of algal and animal life—25 percent of all recognizable, or macro, marine life lives in and around these beautiful environments! Found in clear, tropical oceans, reefs are living structures that are always changing.

Coral reefs are formed when baby coral, or larvae, swim through the water and attach themselves to a rock or another hard surface. The coral will remain there for the rest of its life without moving while it grows a hard skeleton. After the adult coral dies, the skeleton stays in place, creating the foundation for a coral reef!

DESTINATION A.J.

FLIPPERS 'N FINS

Tucked inside Crystal Reef is Flippers 'N Fins, the ocean pet shop. Swim to the door with the seahorse on it to start shopping for an ocean pet! You'll find the fierce anglerfish among other sea creatures here. A visit to the Pet Stop can change your fierce pet to cute, or a cuddly pet to tough. Play around with the different options to see what's offered for each pet. If you create an outfit you love, you can buy it for your pet.

Cool Coral Critters:
The Great Barrier Reef (right) is home to millions of creatures, like these yellow sponges (below), which may look like plants but are actually animals!

Great Barrier Reef

Wonder of the World

THE REAL-LIFE INSPIRATION FOR Crystal Reef and one of the seven wonders of the natural world, the magnificent Great Barrier Reef is larger than the Great Wall of China and is the only living thing on Earth visible from space!

The Great Barrier Reef is not one single reef but a sprawling group of about 3,000 individual reef systems. This biological treasure can be found off the east coast of Queensland, Australia, in the Coral Sea. As countless coral animals died, they left behind their skeletons bound together with algae, which formed the foundation of the reef. As reefs grow only about half an inch (1.3 cm) a year, the more than 1,400-mile (2,253-km)-long Great Barrier Reef took millions of years to form!

Teeming with marine life, the reef is home to over 1,500 species of tropical fish, hundreds of types of birds, and animals like prawns, dolphins, rays, sea turtles, clams, sharks, and crabs. The amazing coral gardens boast more than 400 different kinds of hard corals, the world's largest collection!

This wonder that took millions of years to make is shrinking in only decades! According to a 2012 study, the Great Barrier Reef lost half of its coral over 27 years. Climate change, coastal storms, and crown-of-thorns starfish that feed on coral are to blame. The good news is that if damaged reefs are protected from further harm, they can recover.

ALPHA TIP

COSMO

Some animals can explore both the lands and oceans of Jamaa! Plus, depending on whether you're firmly on the ground or beneath the waves, your actions change. Become a penguin, polar bear, sea otter, or seal and try sleeping, sitting, playing, dancing, or hopping to see what happens!

HELPING REEFS

REEFS PROTECT MILLIONS OF PEOPLE AND ANIMALS.

CORAL REEFS AREN'T ONLY things of beauty. In addition to being home to countless marine species, reefs protect the shoreline and act as a buffer against waves, storms, and floods. Millions of people all over the world depend on these reefs not only for protection, but also for the jobs and food they provide. And like the rain forests they are compared to, coral reefs are home to plants that are being used in new medicines.

Valuable coral reefs all over the world are threatened by many factors. Everyone can do their share to protect these amazing underwater gardens by respecting all guidelines when visiting them. Even if you live thousands of miles away from a reef, you can help out by conserving water, recycling, and not polluting. Learn about reefs, like you're doing right now, and spread the news to your family and friends.

FUN FACT

CLOWNFISH MAKE THEIR HOMES IN ANEMONES' TENTACLES BUT DON'T GET STUNG BY THEM.

Crazy Coral Animals!

Coral reefs are home to some of the most beautiful and bizarre animals in the ocean!

Pygmy Seahorses

Adorable, tiny pygmy sea-horses blend so well into their coral habitats that they're hard for predators to spot.

Moray Eels

Fierce moray eels are often confused with sea snakes. In place of fangs they have supersharp teeth!

Parrotfish

Yuck—snot blankets! Parrotfish wrap themselves up in cocoons of their own mucus while sleeping.

Sea Snakes

Sea snakes have a poisonous bite and are fast swimmers. These aquatic reptiles have to come up for air once every 20 or 30 minutes.

Nudibranchs

These pretty mollusks don't have shells, but they make up for it by being some of the most colorful animals on Earth!

Coral Gobies

These colorful fish are the defenders of a coral reef. They dine on invading seaweeds that threaten the reef's ecosystem.

SO YOU WANT TO BE A

Get ready to have a "shell" time!

ABOUT 110 MILLION YEARS ago, the first sea turtles navigated the Earth's oceans and seas. Today, seven species of sea turtles roam our waters. At up to 2,000 pounds (907 kg) and with a flipper span of 9 feet (2.7 m), leatherback turtles are the largest, but they're tiny compared to the massive turtle *Archelon,* their ancestor. This species grew to be 15 feet (4.6 m) long and weighed as much as 4,000 pounds (1,814 kg), but they went extinct around the time of the dinosaurs.

Yet *Archelon*'s descendants live on! Sea turtles are designed for maneuvering underwater, thanks to their streamlined shells, flippers that act as propellers, and webbed hind feet that work like rudders.

Are You a Sea Turtle?

KNOWN FOR THEIR GRACEFUL SWIMMING AND DETERMINATION WHEN IT COMES TO NESTING, TURTLES ARE THE PERFECT ANIMAL FOR JAMMERS WHO ARE POISED AND STRONG-MINDED!

sea TurTle?

IN tHe FIeLD
WItH **TIerNey THYS**

AMAZING SEA TURTLE NESTS

Every two to four years, female green sea turtles will travel thousands of miles back to the beach where they were born to lay the eggs for the next generation of reptiles.

The largest green sea turtle nesting areas in the Western Hemisphere are in Costa Rica. The female turtles will dig as many as nine nests in one nesting season and will lay between 75 to 200 eggs per nest before covering them with sand and heading back to sea.

After about two months, the eggs will hatch tiny babies. As they rush to get to the sea, the hatchlings face a terrifying gauntlet of seabird predators that are waiting to make a meal out of them.

There are many challenges facing these turtles. Being hunted for their eggs and meat, accidental capture in fishing nets, and disease are some of their biggest threats. To help protect the turtles, people near nesting areas are asked to not disturb nesting sites.

Looking Out:
Like other sea turtles, green sea turtles can't pull their heads into their shells.

STATS

GREEN SEA TURTLE

- ▸ TYPE: Reptile
- ▸ DIET: Sea grasses and algae
- ▸ LIFE SPAN: Over 80 years
- ▸ SIZE: Up to 5 ft (1.5 m)
- ▸ WEIGHT: Up to 700 pounds (318 kg)
- ▸ STATUS: Endangered
- ▸ WHERE THEY LIVE: Europe, North America, coastal waters from Alaska, U.S.A., to Chile

THreatS to ReeFS

CoraLS FiGHt aGainSt Sea Star BLOOMS.

WHILE THE HEALTH OF REEFS ALL OVER the world is threatened by both climate change and pollution, there are also innocent-looking creatures to blame. Crown-of-thorns starfish may be beautiful, but as one of the few animals that feed on living coral tissue they're a huge threat to reefs. These sea stars, which can have as many as 21 arms, are a natural part of the coral reef ecosystem in small numbers. But when conditions in the water cause the population to explode, the sea stars eat corals faster than the corals can grow.

Spreading Fast: Female crown-of-thorns starfish, like this one in the Red Sea, can produce tens of millions of eggs a year.

When sea stars do bloom to excessively high numbers, it's often because of humans. Pollution from farms can flood coastal ocean waters with nutrients that baby sea stars feast on, increasing their population unnaturally. And it's not easy to fix. When an overabundance of crown-of-thorns starfish threatened the Great Barrier Reef in 2003, the Australian government spent millions to try to stop the destructive animals. But the irreplaceable Great Barrier Reef is worth every penny!

Getting Fishy: The Coral Triangle is home to millions of fish like these sweetlips fish (below) and epaulette sharks (right), which uses their fins like legs to walk along the seafloor.

The Coral Triangle

Coral King

ONE REMOTE PART OF THE western Pacific Ocean holds the majority of the world's reef-building corals, almost 600 different species of them. This awesome coral treasure chest was given the name the Coral Triangle, and it boasts 10 times the number of coral species found in the entire Caribbean Sea!

The stunning coral reefs that make up the triangle spread across the waters of Indonesia, Malaysia, the Philippines, Papua New Guinea, Timor-Leste, and the Solomon Islands. Approximately 80 percent of the world's coral species, more than 2,000 species of reef fish, and 6 of the world's 7 marine turtle species can be found in these remarkable underwater gardens.

The Raja Ampat Islands of Indonesia are found in the heart of the Coral Triangle. Raja Ampat means "four kings" but this archipelago, or group of islands,

should have been crowned King of Coral instead! Scientists believe that the reefs in Raja Ampat are the source of coral larvae for the entire Coral Triangle.

The Coral Triangle not only shelters countless fish, sea turtles, barracudas, seahorses, manta rays, and the rare "walking sharks" that use their fins like legs along coral reefs, but is also home to 120 million people. They rely on this marine metropolis for food, protection from storms, and to support themselves economically.

Cool Coral: These mushroom leather and lobed leather corals occupy a pristine reef in Indonesia.

Spot the Differences!

COLORFUL CORALS
DOUBLE TAKE

See if you can spot the 10 differences between these two pictures.

The spectacular array of soft corals and brilliant fish in a coral reef near Fiji in the South Pacific resembles an underwater garden.

FUN FACT

THE BIGGEST LIVING STRUCTURE ON EARTH IS AUSTRALIA'S GREAT BARRIER REEF.

Find the answers on page 264.

PET STOP

EARS UP

GREAT GAMES
IN CRYSTAL REEF

KANI COVE

SPLASH INTO KANI COVE TO EXPLORE THE RUINS OF A SHIP LOST BENEATH THE WAVES.

WARNING: THAR BE PIRATE TREASURE HERE! AS YOU explore, make sure to swim into the sunken ship's hull. Riches can be found for the taking in Sunken Treasures. Pick up some plunder for your ocean den here!

Pirates aren't the only thing you need to keep a lookout for in Kani Cove. While you may spot gentle manatees, colorful parrotfish, or tiny shrimp, hammerhead sharks also roam the waters here.

IN THE FIELD WITH TIERNEY THYS

HUNTING FOR TREASURE

Many treasure hunters hope to make a big profit by discovering priceless artifacts. About three million shipwrecks are thought to lie on the ocean floor. Searching for these has become big business, as companies are popping up to try to cash in on the ocean's treasures.

Hunting for shipwrecks is not easy. It's also very expensive. Some deep-sea explorations can cost up to $30 million! Yet it can pay off. But digging carelessly can destroy underwater archaeological sites. That's why the United Nations Educational, Scientific, and Cultural Organization (UNESCO) is encouraging governments, educators, and private businesses to work together to preserve the underwater cultural heritage of the world.

Sea Cow: Manatees may seem sluggish, but they can swim up to 15 miles an hour (25 km/h) in short bursts.

If you see any of these creatures, be sure to add them to your Journey Book!

There's a lot of exploring to do underwater! People who study and excavate these underwater shipwrecks are called maritime or nautical archaeologists. Maritime archaeologists also study ancient voyages, seafaring, and ships. Humans have been voyaging on the open seas for thousands of years. Lots of valuable evidence of sea travel can be found in our massive oceans, but as much as 95 percent of the world's ocean and 99 percent of the ocean floor are unexplored. Just imagine the wonders waiting to be discovered beneath the sea!

Pinning Prey: Hammerheads use their unusually shaped head to pin their favorite food, stingrays, to the seafloor.

Famous Bow: The *Titanic*'s bow is now covered in rust.

Stately Room: A light shows the interior of a first-class cabin.

THE LARGEST MARITIME DISASTER in peacetime history occurred on April 15, 1912, when the luxury ocean liner R.M.S. *Titanic* sank into the icy depths of the North Atlantic Ocean. On her first voyage, the British ship hit an enormous iceberg. The *Titanic*, touted as "unsinkable," disappeared beneath the waves in less than three hours, costing the lives of 1,500 men, women, and children.

The ship's exact whereabouts remained a mystery until 1985, when oceanographer Robert Ballard discovered it about 560 miles (900 km) off the south coast of Newfoundland, Canada, using a submersible robot called Argo. Private salvage companies immediately went to work to gather artifacts from the sunken ship, until laws were passed making it illegal to remove anything from the wreckage without official approval. Expensive clothing, jewelry, perfumes, shoes, reading glasses, and fixtures from the ship, such as lights, signs, windows, and even toilets, are among the items recovered.

Underwater cinematographers traveled 13,000 feet (3,962 m) to the ocean floor to capture haunting video of the *Titanic* in its watery grave. The tragic sinking of this great ship has inspired songs, movies, plays, and a fascination that still exists 100 years later.

Today, the *Titanic* is fighting another losing battle: time. The huge ship is an ocean-floor buffet for marine organisms. The wood of the ship has been eaten by mollusks while microscopic bacteria and fungi munch away on the metal hull. As they eat, they create rust icicles, which now cover the *Titanic*'s bow. But oceanographers are working on ideas for how to preserve this piece of history.

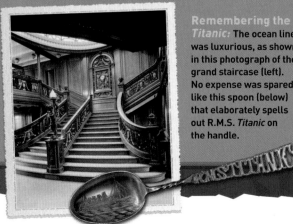

Remembering the *Titanic*: The ocean liner was luxurious, as shown in this photograph of the grand staircase (left). No expense was spared, like this spoon (below) that elaborately spells out R.M.S. *Titanic* on the handle.

FINDING SHIPWRECKS

UNDISCOVERED SHIPWRECKS and lost treasure have an air of excitement and romance about them. They allow a person's imagination to wander and have been the subject of countless tales. But there's a downside to these underwater relics.

Military ships, cargo vessels, pirate ships, and tankers transporting everything from oil to chemicals have sunk to the bottom of the ocean. Many of them could potentially be leaking pollutants into the sea.

Thirty-six sunken ships off the coast of the United States were identified by the National Oceanic and Atmospheric Administration (NOAA) as posing a threat of oil pollution. Knowing where these ships are can help cleanup efforts if a spill is reported in the area.

Amazing Shipwreck Treasures

Here are just some of the treasures that have been discovered beneath the ocean waves!

Show off a little shipwreck bling! These beautiful baubles, made of diamond, sapphire, and ruby, were found in the wreckage of a Spanish galleon.

The mysterious Antikythera mechanism, recovered from a shipwreck off the coast of Greece, is 2,000 years old and contains 30 different types of interlocking gears. Today archaeologists believe it's an astronomical calendar.

An incredible $36 million worth of silver was found off the coast of Ireland in the S.S. *Gairsoppa*. This British cargo ship was torpedoed by a Nazi U-boat during World War II.

Pirate Leader: An illustration shows Captain Bartholomew Roberts with his two ships the *Royal Fortune* and the *Ranger*.

Pirates!

Ahoy, Matey!

PIRATES HAVE BEEN around for thousands of years. Ever since humans figured out how to transport valuables by water they've been plagued by pirates!

The way to the most infamous age in piracy was paved by Queen Elizabeth I of England. Dubbed the "Pirate Queen" by her enemies, she asked her best sailors to become privateers and loaned them ships and supplies to attack boats from other countries, especially Spain. The queen split the spoils with her pirates, such as famous privateers Sir Walter Raleigh and Sir Francis Drake. Everyone was happy—except for the Spaniards,

Royal Jaws: Elizabeth I had black teeth.

that is. They were definitely not pleased.

But why share the loot when you can keep it all for yourself? During the first quarter of the 1700s, dubbed the "golden age of piracy," thousands made a living by becoming pirates. This is when famous pirates like Blackbeard, Major Stede Bonnet, Captain "Calico Jack" Rackham, and Bartholomew "Black Bart" Roberts ruled the seas!

Cheers! Salvagers found 168 unbroken bottles of champagne in a wreck in the Baltic Sea from the 1820s. One bottle alone sold for $37,400—and the champagne's still drinkable!

The sea was paved with gold! A 1622 wreck of a Spanish ship, the *Atocha*, dropped over 185,000 silver and 120 gold coins along the ocean floor.

So you want to Be a Shark?

WHY MESS WITH PERFECTION? SHARKS HAVE EXISTED on Earth for 400 million years and have changed little in the past 200 million. Their ancient design allows for speed and maneuverability coupled with a super sense of smell. Sharks are super-powerful predators.

But there's no need to skip that ocean vacation with your family. Very few species of sharks attack humans. In 2016, only 81 unprovoked shark attacks were reported worldwide. The odds of being bitten by a shark are 1 in 11.5 million!

Earth's oceans are home to approximately 500 species of sharks. These range from dwarf lantern sharks, which are only eight inches (20 cm) long, to enormous, 40-foot (12-m)-long whale sharks, the largest fish in the sea!

Are You a Shark?

IF YOU LIKE TO SNIFF YOUR FOOD BEFORE YOU EAT IT AND HAVE A KILLER SMILE, THE SHARK IS THE PERFECT JAMAA ANIMAL FOR YOU!

POWER SNIFFERS

Sharks have some of the most sophisticated snouts in the area. Great whites can smell blood from miles away. The scent organs in their snouts have amazing sniffing abilities. In fact, the part of sharks' brains dedicated to smell, or olfaction, is unusually large compared with other animals.

Blood isn't the only thing these sharks can detect. Thanks to amazing organs called ampullae of Lorenzini, sharks can sense when another animal's muscles are contracting! The

Shark Senses: Ampullae of Lorenzini look like small black dots on sharks' snouts.

ampullae, located in their snouts, help sharks sense electromagnetic fields.

STATS

GREAT WHITE SHARK

- ▸ **TYPE:** Fish
- ▸ **DIET:** Sea lions, seals, small-toothed whales, sea turtles, and carrion (dead and decaying animals)
- ▸ **LIFE SPAN:** 30 years
- ▸ **SIZE:** 15 feet (4.6 m) to more than 20 feet (6 m)
- ▸ **WEIGHT:** 5,000 pounds (2,268 kg) or more
- ▸ **STATUS:** Endangered
- ▸ **WHERE THEY LIVE:** Nearly all of the world's oceans and seas, mostly temperate coastal areas

Taking a Whiff: Great white sharks poke their heads out of the water to pick up airborne scents.

FUN FACT

GREAT WHITE SHARKS HAVE THE LARGEST TEETH OF ALL LIVING SHARKS— TWO INCHES (5 CM) LONG!

Studying Shipwrecks

Preserved wrecks are a look back in time.

A SINKING SHIP WAS AN unlucky thing for anyone who happened to be on board! But for historians, the remains of these underwater disasters are often a fortunate gift. Well-preserved shipwrecks serve as time capsules, giving a rare glimpse into the past. When conditions are right, such as cold water and little marine life, some of these ships and their cargo can remain perfectly preserved.

In 2012, an amazingly well-preserved shipwreck was found in the Gulf of Mexico. Muskets and cannons were discovered with the wreck, leading researchers to speculate that the ship possibly belonged to pirates!

PIRATE MYTHS

PIRATES MADE THEIR PRISONERS (OR EACH OTHER) WALK THE PLANK.

Forcing someone to walk the plank and plunge into the ocean was an uncommon practice. Pirates will forever be associated with it thanks to two fictional tales: *Treasure Island* by Robert Louis Stevenson and *Peter Pan* by J. M. Barrie. The truth is that pirate punishments were a lot more gruesome. Pirate justice included whipping, torture, marooning, and keelhauling, a practice in which a pirate bound to a rope was dragged down one side of the ship, underneath it, and then up the other side.

ALL PIRATES WERE MEN.

Not true! Ferocious female pirates Anne Bonny and Mary Read were respected by their crews for both their toughness and their fighting skills.

PIRATES BURIED THEIR TREASURE.

Once a ship was plundered or a town looted, pirates wanted their share pronto! Spoils were quickly divided and rarely hidden or buried. Again, this piece of popular pirate lore is thanks to the novel *Treasure Island*.

PIRATES DON'T EXIST ANYMORE.

As long as people continue to travel by water, there will be pirates. In 2012, 297 ships were attacked by pirates. Most of these attacks took place off the coasts of East and West Africa.

seek and find

UNDERSEA SEARCH

CAN YOU FIND THE OBJECTS IN THIS WATERY SCENE? LOOK CAREFULLY!

2	anchors	1	sea turtle
7	sea stars	5	clownfish
2	hammerhead sharks	3	seahorses
		2	lobsters
1	moray eel	2	diving flippers
6	seashells		

Find the answers on page 264.

DEEP BLUE

AS YOU SWIM DEEPER, BE PREPARED TO SEE THE MOST UNUSUAL CREATURES IN THE WORLD!

P LUNGING INTO THE DEEPEST WATERS OF JAMAA'S oceans, you'll be greeted by eerie squid and translucent jellies! The lack of sunlight at the bottom of ocean trenches like Deep Blue means the animals live in an almost pitch-black environment, causing many of them to lack color and to develop other odd physical characteristics. Instead of making you feel as if you are miles underneath the water, these bizarre organisms can make you believe you're on another planet!

Prepare to Dive: This submersible, called DeepSee, is used by filmmakers and is capable of carrying three people to depths of 1,500 feet (457 m).

As you dive even farther into these quiet, gloomy waters you may even stumble across some treasure!

Most ocean trenches are located in the largest ecosystem on Earth, the deep sea. Trenches are long, deep depressions carved into the ocean floor. The movement of tectonic plates is what forms these marine chasms. The deepest parts of the oceans, and in fact, of the entire Earth, are found in ocean trenches. They range from 24,000 feet (7.3 km) to 36,000 feet (11 km) deep.

IN THE FIELD WITH TIERNEY THYS

DIVING DEEP

Exploring the ocean is tricky. One of the most obvious reasons is that people cannot breathe underwater! The first snorkel was a hollow reed early swimmers used to breathe air. Diving suits and air pumps paved the way for modern scuba-diving gear. That solved one problem. But the deeper divers wanted to go, the more intense the water pressure.

High water pressure during deep-water dives can put stress on the body that can injure the heart and lungs, but there are a number of ways divers can adjust to these pressure changes safely. No ordinary gear can be used to explore the extreme depths of the ocean. Submarines and robots let us explore the very bottom.

Studies of the deep ocean are important because this environment can help us research life's origins as well as earthquakes that cause deadly tsunamis.

Alien Life: This small plankton (left) and long red-lined sea cucumbers can be found in the deep ocean.

YOU'LL HAVE to dive deep, deep underneath the waves to explore one of the most remote and strangest places on Earth: the Mariana Trench!

Located in the western Pacific Ocean, this crescent-shaped trench has a depth of 36,201 feet (11,034 m)—more than 6 miles (9.7 km) deep! It's also five times the length of the Grand Canyon and spans 43 miles (69 km) wide. If Mount Everest, the tallest mountain in the world, were dropped into the Mariana Trench, its peak would still be more than a mile (1.6 km) underwater. Thousands of climbers have scaled Mount Everest, yet only three people have been able to descend into the deepest part of the Mariana Trench.

The Mariana Trench was discovered by the H.M.S. *Challenger* in 1875 during the first global oceanographic cruise. The depths of the trench were plumbed again by the *Challenger II* in 1951. The deepest part of the trench, Challenger Deep, was named after these pioneering vessels. Descents into the trench took place in 1960 and 2012.

Aquatic life-forms inhabit the trench at different depths, including shrimp-like amphipods, translucent holothurians or sea cucumbers, anglerfish, and eels. Life at the bottom of Challenger Deep used to be thought of as scarce. That's because the water pressure here is like having 50 jumbo jets piled on top of you! Yet some of the world's earliest forms of life, single-celled organisms called foraminifera, are thriving in great numbers in the seafloor here.

Mariana Trench

Deepest Place on Earth

	SEA LEVEL
Deepest scuba dive	
Deepest recorded sperm whale dive	10,000 ft. 3,048 m
H.M.S. *Titanic* wreckage	15,000 ft. 4,572 m
	20,000 ft. 6,096 m
	25,000 ft. 7,620 m
Height of Mount Everest	30,000 ft. 9,144 m
Challenger Deep	35,000 ft. 10,668 m

So you want to Be an

MONSTERS OF THE DEEP, intelligent sea creatures, or delicious delicacies? Found in oceans throughout the world, octopuses are known for their bulging eyes, rounded body, and of course their eight limbs! They also have an awesome swimming stunt. Octopuses can swim backward by blasting water through a tube on their bodies called a siphon.

Octopuses are mollusks like clams, oysters, and snails. The smallest octopuses, the *O. arborescens* species, are only about two inches (5 cm) long. On the other side of the spectrum are giant Pacific octopuses. The biggest one ever recorded was 30 feet (9.1 m) long and weighed over 600 pounds (272 kg)!

IN the FieLD With TIerNey THYS

EXPERT ESCAPE ARTISTS

Octopuses are stealthy marine animals that are very ninja-like in the way they evade predators and disappear into their surroundings.

To escape detection, octopuses can change their color to gray, brown, pink, blue, or green to blend in with their surroundings.

Many times hungry hunters will pass right by octopuses without even seeing them! If seals or sharks don't spot them, octopuses can shoot out an inky fluid and make a getaway. They can also tuck themselves into small places where predators can't reach them. And if

Atlantic white-spotted octopus

something does manage to chomp down on one of the octopus's eight arms, a new one will grow back. That's arm-azing!

OCTOPUS?

Get ready to lend a hand to all your buddies!

Supersmarts:
Octopuses are smart and can open jars, mimic other octopuses, and even solve puzzles!

STATS

GIANT PACIFIC OCTOPUS

- ▶ TYPE: Invertebrate
- ▶ DIET: Shrimp, clams, lobsters, fish, sharks, and seabirds
- ▶ LIFE SPAN: 3 to 5 years
- ▶ SIZE: 9.8 to 16 feet (3 to 5 m)
- ▶ WEIGHT: 22 to 110 pounds (10 to 50 kg)
- ▶ WHERE THEY LIVE: Temperate water of the Pacific, from southern California to Alaska, U.S.A., west to the Aleutian Islands and Japan

Are You an Octopus?

KNOWN FOR THEIR INTELLIGENCE AND STEALTH, THIS IS A GREAT ANIMAL FOR SMART JAMMERS WHO HAVE NINJA SKILLS!

MONSTERS OF THE DEEP

TO SURVIVE IN THE DEEPEST place on Earth, deep-sea organisms have to adapt to total darkness, crushing pressures, and cold-water temperatures.

Living in the dark means that many organisms that live in the deep sea lack color or are transparent. Some look like they could be aliens from another world!

Many of these animals feast on decaying microbes, algae, plants, and dead animals from the upper zones of the ocean that have sunk to the bottom. When hagfish come across carcasses, they burrow into them and then eat the decaying corpses from the inside out!

Another unique adaptation of ocean trench animals is deep-sea gigantism. Most famous are elusive giant squid. The biggest one ever recorded was 43 feet (13 m) long and may have weighed nearly a ton (0.9 t)!

Deep-Sea Creatures

Meet some of the deep-sea denizens that live in ocean trenches. Scientists believe that many more unusual animals are just waiting to be discovered in these vast unexplored areas of the world!

▲ Anglerfish

The appendages that stick over anglerfishes' mouths are dorsal spines that they use as fishing poles! The tip of this spine is bioluminescent, or glowing, and acts as a lure to attract smaller fish.

Hatchetfish

Built-in night-lights! The organs that line the belly of these bizarre-looking fish glow as bright as daylight and are used to confuse predators.

Alien Deep: Below, crabs crawl over *Riftia* tubes growing on hydrothermal vents. At right, deep-sea vents spew minerals that form when the hot fluid mixes with seawater.

Hydrothermal Vents

Deep-Sea Smokers

THE GEYSERS OF THE OCEAN floor are hydrothermal vents. Hot water is pushed out through the vents as seawater circulates through volcanic rocks. As a result, these deep-sea smokers emit warm, mineral-rich water that contains iron, copper, zinc, and hydrogen sulfide.

This mineral concoction works as a substitute for sunlight to the organisms that live in the deep sea. They can't use photosynthesis, the process by which plants make energy from sunlight that most life on Earth depends on. Instead, the vents allow chemosynthesis to take place. It's a process that organisms use to make food without needing sunlight.

Chemosynthesis makes hydrothermal vents a popular place to live in the deep sea! Thriving chemical-based communities surround these vents, and it's the only system on Earth where life can flourish with zero sunlight. The life that is supported here includes tube worms, fish, crabs, octopuses, snails, and clams.

Scientists believe these amazing environments could be the birthplace where life on Earth began! The reaction between the salty ocean water and the chemicals produced from hydrothermal vents might have paved the way for the first biological molecules on the planet.

Viperfish

Viperfishes' jagged, needlelike teeth are so big that these fish can't close their mouths. They use glowing organs in their bodies to lure prey.

Giant Squid

Giant squids' eyeballs are the same size as beach balls! Those huge eyes help these creatures see in the murky waters they live in.

Gulper Eels

Gulper eels get their names from their enormous mouths, and some have mouths longer than their bodies. Their stomachs can expand, allowing these eels to eat food bigger than they are.

Off the Deep END

HOW MUCH DO YOU KNOW ABOUT THE DEEPEST PARTS OF THE SEA? QUIZ YOURSELF TO FIND OUT!

#1 Which of these is on the ocean floor and spans the entire planet?

a. an underwater mountain range
b. a very deep trench
c. a coral reef
d. a chain of sea stars holding hands

#3 If you were at the deepest point of the ocean, the weight of the water pushing down on you would feel most like _____.

a. a person
b. a car
c. an airplane
d. 50 airplanes

#4 Tube worms living near super-hot vents eat what to survive?

a. crabs boiled by the vents
b. giant squid attracted to the vents
c. poisonous gas spewing from the vents
d. fish tacos from the nearest snack shack

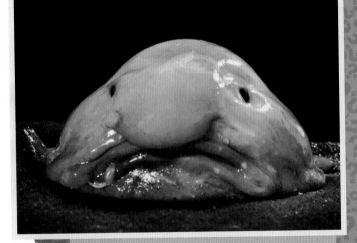

#2 Blobfish, found at depths of more than 3,000 feet (914 m), have been voted the world's ugliest creature.
True or false?

#5
Bioluminescence is a phenomenon that occurs only in fish.
True or false?

#6 Scientists were shocked to discover that life on the ocean floor could exist without
_____.

a. oxygen
b. food
c. gravity
d. Internet access

#8 Spider crabs living on the ocean floor can grow up to how wide?

a. 1 foot (0.3 m)   **c.** 12 feet (3.6 m)
b. 3 feet (0.9 m)   **d.** 20 feet (6 m)

#9 Deep-sea jellyfish will use flashy lights when attacked by other fish in order to
_____.

a. scare the fish
b. blind the fish
c. attract predators to eat the fish
d. convince the fish it was a lightbulb

#10 What is the name given to the deepest part of the ocean?

a. Bikini Bottom
b. Mariana Trench
c. Champion Deep
d. Davy Jones's Locker

#7 What did scientists discover on the ocean floor 1,000 miles (1,600 km) east of Japan?

a. the world's deepest canyon
b. the world's largest volcano
c. the world's tallest mountain
d. the world's largest Godzilla footprint

PHANTOM'S TREASURE

LOOK FOR THIS GREAT GAME
IN DEEP BLUE

Find the answers on page 265.

MT. SHIVEER

Get ready to climb the HIGHEST MOUNTAIN in Jamaa!

HERE YOU CAN LET YOUR INNER EXPLORER PLAY WILD! Once you've made it to the top of Mt. Shiveer, get back to the bottom by whooshing down the ice slide. All that snow and ice is chilling, but there are plenty of places to warm up here. Take a dip in the natural hot springs, or head into the Hot Cocoa Hut to get toasty warm with a hot beverage or by shopping for some cozy winter clothes.

Snowcapped Peaks: The sun rises over Cerro Torre mountain in Argentina's Andes mountain range.

Rocky cliffs, little vegetation, and extreme temperature changes make this environment a place where only the strong survive. No animals or vegetation can live at the very top of high mountains like Mount Everest. Yet in the lower levels of the Himalayan mountain range, and in the surrounding forests and valleys, you can find bears, leopards, wolves, wild boar, yaks, and hoofed animals like muntjacs, serow, and tahr.

To be a mountain, you've got to be tall! Mountains are pieces of land that rise significantly higher than the area around them. When

Mountain Animals: Yaks (above), wild boar (above right), and common tahr (right) live in the Himalaya.

a piece of protruding land rises over 2,000 feet (610 m) tall, it's usually considered a mountain.

Both people and animals make their homes in mountain ranges around the world. It's not an easy place to live, especially the higher you climb.

PECK

ALPHA TIP

When you visit Mt. Shiveer, you might find yourself on thin ice—literally! Many Jammers like to go and stand on the frozen pond with the caution sign. They'll even start jumping up and down on it! The ice will crack, but has never completely broken ... yet!

Top of the World: Sherpas play horseshoes underneath Tibetan prayer flags on Mount Everest (right). An aerial view of the mountain (below) shows its massive size.

Mount Everest
High Hopes

IMAGINE THE 103-FLOOR EMPIRE State Building stacked on top of itself 20 times! This fantastic height is the same as that of the world's highest summit, and real-life inspiration for Mt. Shiveer, Mount Everest. It towers in the Himalaya of southern Asia at 29,035 feet (8,850 m). Located on the border of Nepal and Tibet, this mystical mountain has been beckoning explorers to climb its lofty heights for decades.

Even before the rest of the world started beating a path to the base of Mount Everest, it was home to the Sherpas who live on the southern side of the mountain. They have adapted to the high altitude and cold of mountain life. They've helped lead almost every climbing expedition on Mount Everest.

Eventually, European mountaineers arrived on the scene. George Mallory discovered the northern approach to the mighty mountain in 1921. He's responsible for the famous line "Because it's there" when asked why he wanted to climb Mount Everest. He would never make it to the top. While trying to reach the summit in 1924, Mallory died.

He's not the only one to perish scaling the harshest, tallest mountain in the world. Climbing the mountain is dangerous due to harsh temperatures, avalanches, blizzards, and lack of oxygen.

The first people to successfully reach the summit were Edmund Hillary and Sherpa Tenzing Norgay on May 29, 1953. As long as Mount Everest continues rising high into the sky, there will be people who will want to scale this magnificent mountain. Why? Because it's there!

High Climbers: Sherpa Tenzing Norgay (left) and Edmund Hillary (right) reached Mount Everest's summit in 1953.

MOUNT EVEREST IS THE HEIGHT OF MORE THAN 20 EMPIRE STATE BUILDINGS!

SO YOU WANT TO BE AN EAGLE?

STATS

BALD EAGLE

- TYPE: Bird
- DIET: Fish, small mammals
- LIFE SPAN: Up to 28 years
- SIZE: Up to 43 inches (109 cm); wingspan, up to 8 feet (2.4 m)
- WEIGHT: 6.5 to 14 pounds (3 to 6.5 kg)
- WHERE THEY LIVE: North America

IN THE FIELD WITH DR. BRADY BARR

PROTECTING BALD EAGLES

These birds prove that when people protect endangered animals they can be saved!

When bald eagles were first named the national bird of America, they numbered up to 100,000. Hunting and a pesticide called DDT dropped the number of bald eagles to only about 450 nesting pairs by the 1960s. But when the use of DDT was banned in 1972, the number of bald eagles began to rise again.

By 2007, over 9,700 nesting pairs were counted in the wild and bald eagles were removed from the endangered species list!

Take to the Skies!

STRONG AND MAJESTIC, EAGLES have been a symbol of power for many years. The Greeks and Romans used these birds of strength on their coins and medals. Bald eagles have been the national symbol of the United States of America since 1782.

The term "eagle" is applied to birds of prey that are more powerful than buzzards or hawks and that feed mainly on live animals, rather than scavenging on carrion, or animals that are already dead.

Swooping quickly down from above, eagles use the element of surprise to catch their prey off-guard. Many eagles are also fantastic fishers and can spy fish in the water up to a mile (1.6 km) away!

Bald eagles build their nests, or aeries, at the top of tall trees or cliffs with branches and twigs. These birds build big! One of the largest nests ever found was 9 feet (2.7 m) wide and 20 feet (6.1 m) deep and weighed more than 4,000 pounds (1,814 kg)!

Are You an Eagle?
POWERFUL AND FAST EAGLES ARE PERFECT ANIMALS FOR JAMMERS WHO ARE STRONG AND SPEEDY!

Growing Up Bald: It takes about five years for young bald eagles to reach adulthood and have completely white heads and tails.

Mountains and People

LIVING HIGH UP TOGETHER!

King of the Mountain

To make it up high, you've got to be mighty! Animals need special skills to live in mountainous terrain. Check out how these animals survive.

Cool Kicks

Athletic sneakers have got nothing on the incredible footwear sported by hoofed animals that live in rocky regions! Mountain goats, llamas, and ibex have specially designed feet that help them move easily along rocky ground.

Fur and Furnaces

Many mountain animals, like yaks and alpacas, have thick fur coats to protect them against frigid temperatures. The rumen, a chamber of yaks' stomachs, can heat up to 104°F (40°C), keeping these animals warm.

It's in Their Blood

Llamas have a unique way of dealing with the lack of oxygen. Their blood contains a very high concentration of red blood cells, which helps deliver more oxygen throughout their bodies!

Tough Teeth

The sparse vegetation in some areas of the mountain is tough and hard to eat. To chow down, many herbivores have big and sturdy chompers.

MOUNTAINS AREN'T EASY TO CLIMB OR live on, but humans have been reaping the rewards of these hilly environments throughout time.

On fertile mountain slopes in Java, Guatemala, and Sicily, people grow tea and coffee in lower zones and graze cattle on the rich grass found higher up. Mountains provide fresh water, timber, and minerals, as well as beautiful and scenic vacation spots. But the risk of doing business in some mountain landscapes is avalanches and landslides!

Mountain ranges can also act like natural security walls. High mountains bordering Switzerland have protected it from attacks and involvement in several wars. In order to attack Rome, Hannibal, the military leader of Carthage, had to make a treacherous trek across the Alps in 218 B.C. with thousands of troops, horses, and about 40 elephants—no easy feat!

DESTINATION A.J.

HOT COCOA HUT

After taking an exhilarating zip down Mt. Shiveer's ice slide, cozy up with a warm drink at the Hot Cocoa Hut. Inside the colorful tent you can choose a delicious warm beverage made with your choice of toppings. Curl up on one of the comfy blankets scattered around the room as you listen to the wind blow outside. Or do a little shopping here at the Shiveer Shoppe and pick out a winter outfit that will protect you from Mt. Shiveer's icy weather!

SO YOU WANT TO BE A SNOW LEOPARD?

SHOW OFF YOUR *PURR*-FECTION!

IN THE FIELD WITH GABBY WILD

HELPING SNOW LEOPARDS

Snow leopards are endangered, but they have a lot of friends looking out for them! In Tibet, snow leopards' territories are shared by many Buddhist monasteries. It turns out the monks who live there are great neighbors to these beautiful cats! They go out on patrols to protect the snow leopards from potential poachers. The monks are also educating other people in the area about why it's important not to harm these animals.

IT'S EASY TO SEE HOW THESE BIG CATS GOT THEIR nickname, "ghost cat." Unlike darker leopards, snow leopards are a lighter gray color with less distinctive, almost blurry, spots, and a snow white stomach. The effect is beautiful as well as helpful. Snow leopards live in the mountains of Central Asia and India, and their coats help them blend into their snowy and rocky surroundings.

Snow leopards' coats are also thick and dense, creating a natural insulation against the cold temperatures. These cats have built-in snowshoes, thanks to their furry feet, which help give traction on slippery surfaces.

But snow leopards are endangered due to poaching and habitat decline. Scientists are working on learning more about these rare and elusive creatures, to figure out the best ways to protect them.

STATS

SNOW LEOPARD

▸ **TYPE:** Mammal
▸ **DIET:** Blue sheep (bharal), ibex, marmots, hares, and game birds
▸ **LIFE SPAN:** 20 years (in captivity)
▸ **SIZE:** 4 to 5 feet (1.2 to 1.5 m); tail, 36 inches (91 cm)
▸ **WEIGHT:** 60 to 120 pounds (27 to 54 kg)
▸ **STATUS:** Endangered
▸ **WHERE THEY LIVE:** Asia

Are You a Snow Leopard?

IF THE SNOW LEOPARD IS THE ANIMAL FOR YOU, YOU'RE MOST LIKELY THE KIND OF JAMMER WHO ALWAYS WINS AT GAMES OF HIDE AND SEEK! LIKE THE ELUSIVE SNOW LEOPARD, YOU LIKE BEING ALONE.

Cozy Tails:
Snow leopards use their tails like blankets in really cold weather.

MAKING A MOUNTAIN

THE POPULAR SAYING IS TRUE— mountains can be made out of molehills! Or rocks, dirt, twigs, or anything else on the ground when the Earth's plates collide!

Earth's outer layer is made up of plates called the lithosphere. When plates underneath landmasses move and collide, the crust of the earth crumbles and buckles to form mountain ranges. The mountains found on our planet are evidence of the plates moving long ago. The Himalaya began to be formed 45 million years ago during a collision of continental plates. To this day, the plates that slid underneath each other to form this mountain range are still slowly moving, growing the mountains by millimeters each year!

IN tHE FiELD
WiTH Dr. BRADY BARR

MOUNTAIN MONSTER

A powerful and giant creature, towering over six feet (2 m) tall and covered with brown, matted hair. Is the yeti, or the abominable snowman, fact or fiction?

No one has ever been able to prove the existence of this wild man of the mountain. Sightings of large footprints in the snow and of a beast walking on two legs have been reported for years in the Himalayan mountains.

Nonbelievers offer this explanation: bears. But a lack of evidence doesn't deter die-hard yeti fanatics. Even in modern times, new species are discovered in rain forests and the oceans all the time. The vast majority of the Himalaya are unexplored with no one living there. If such a creature as the yeti did exist, wouldn't this mountain range be the perfect place for it to hide? One can only imagine!

Arctic Headgear: Musk oxen (below) have horns, which males use to compete for mates; walruses (right) have ivory tusks, which males use to protect their females and to pull themselves out of the water!

The Arctic

The Top of the World

EVER FEEL LIKE YOU'RE ON THE top of the world? People use that expression when they're feeling happy. But it would be more accurate to say when you're feeling cold!

That's because the northernmost part of the world, the North Pole, is surrounded by a vast and icy area known as the Arctic. Most of the Arctic is covered with ocean and floating sea ice. The majority of the land in the Arctic is in the Arctic Circle, which runs parallel to the Equator, and is found in Asia, Europe, and North America. The Arctic Circle encompasses 6 percent of the total surface area of the Earth. The land in the Arctic Circle is tundra, which is marked by cold temperatures; dry, powerful winds; and permanently frozen soil called permafrost.

Jamaa's Mt. Shiveer is based on the Arctic's chilly climes. Even though this inhospitable place contains less wildlife than other habitats of the world, life still exists here. Polar bears and arctic foxes hunt, caribou and musk oxen graze on the sparse grasses, and small collared lemmings hibernate in the permafrost. In the Arctic Ocean, whales, polar bears, walruses, seals, and sharks roam the waters and coasts.

It's hard to imagine people living in this hostile land, but societies were built around the hunting and fishing that this region of the world offers. The Inuit people are just one of dozens of native peoples of the Arctic.

Today, weather and polar research stations are found in the Arctic where glaciologists study the ice and snow, biologists investigate climate change, oceanographers explore the mysteries of the ocean, and astronomers look to the skies!

SO YOU WANT TO BE AN
Arctic Fox?

BLEND IN ON THE ICE!

STATS

ARCTIC FOX

▸ TYPE: Mammal
▸ DIET: Lemmings, seal, crabs, and plants
▸ LIFE SPAN: 3 to 6 years
▸ SIZE: Head and body, 18 to 26.8 inches
  (46 to 68 cm); tail, up to 13.8 inches
  (35 cm)
▸ WEIGHT: 6.5 to 17 pounds (3 to 8 kg)
▸ STATUS: Least concern
▸ WHERE THEY LIVE: Arctic tundra

NO MATTER THE SEASON, THERE'S a good chance you won't see arctic foxes, even if skulks of them were standing right in front of you! That's because these animals' fur changes with the seasons, from white or gray in the snowy winter to grayish brown to match the tundra come spring. The camouflage this provides allows them to hunt with stealth, which is critical for their survival, especially during the long winters when food is scarce.

Their thick fur also helps to keep them warm on the frigid Arctic tundra where the temperatures can fall as low as minus 58°F (-50°C). These clever foxes also have extra warmth in their tails, which they will wrap around themselves like a blanket for much needed insulation within the hollows they dig out in the snow.

Ancient Homes: Some arctic fox dens are 300 years old.

Are You an Arctic Fox?

THIS IS A GREAT ANIMAL FOR JAMMERS WHO AREN'T AFRAID TO BRAVE THE COLD BUT ALSO LOVE TO HUNKER DOWN. IF YOU ARE BOTH HARDY AND CUDDLY, THEN YOU MIGHT BE AN ARCTIC FOX!

BOBCAT

▸ TYPE: Mammal
▸ DIET: Rabbits, rodents, birds,
and other small game
▸ LIFE SPAN: 10 to 16 years
▸ WEIGHT: 22 to 44 pounds
(10 to 20 kg)

▸ SIZE: Head and body, 26 to 41
inches (66 to 104 cm); tail,
4 to 7 inches (10 to 18 cm)
▸ STATUS: Least concern
▸ WHERE THEY LIVE: North
America

... or a LYNX?

Sneak Like a cat!

LYNX ARE THE MOST mysterious of cats. They are renowned for their stealth—on huge, furry, paws they creep through the night, looking for snowshoe hare, mice, squirrels, birds, and deer. Their paws are really, really big—though lynx are five times smaller than cougars, their feet are the same size. Lynx have tufts of fur on their ears, too, which act like antennae to aid their already excellent hearing. They also have stellar eyesight: Lynx can spot mice from 250 feet (75 m) away! And don't forget their powerful hind legs— lynx can leap as far as 21 feet (6 m) in a single bound. This makes lynx some of the savviest hunters around. They even can take down a deer four times their size.

Are You a Lynx?

IF YOU'RE THE TYPE OF PERSON WHO PREFERS PEACE AND QUIET, YOU'VE GOT A LOT IN COMMON WITH THE LYNX. THIS IS A GREAT ANIMAL FOR JAMMERS WHO ARE SPEEDY AND SOLITARY!

seek and FiND

AWESOME Arctic

CAN YOU FIND the OBJECTS IN this POLAR SCENE? LOOK CAREFULLY!

1	snowman	3	walruses
5	caribou	4	harp seals
10	people	2	snowy owls
10	polar bears	3	arctic hares
6	orcas (killer whales)	6	snowflakes

HOT COCOA MACHINE

GEM BREAKER

Great GaMeS
IN MT. SHIVEER

Find the answers on page 265.

Kimbara
OUTBACK

A DRY, DUSTY WIND WHIPS AGAINST YOUR FACE AS YOU STEP ONTO THE SUN-BAKED GROUND OF THE WILD OUTBACK!

R

UGGED ROCK FORMATIONS SURROUND YOU. A WATERFALL courses down a rocky cliff, and you stop to take a dip in the cool water. Feeling refreshed, you climb onto the bridge to soak in the sweeping panoramas of deserts and grasslands. Strange birds, unlike any you've ever seen, run away as you approach. You have a feeling you're going to see a lot more wacky animals and plants as you explore Kimbara Outback!

Rock Life: Australia's rock canyons, like this Kings Canyon rock wall (right), have been home to many animals, such as this thorny devil (below right), for millions of years.

OUTBACK IMPORTS

You'll find the rugged Outback Imports carved into a rocky cliff on top of Kimbara Outback's waterfalls. Durable den items built to last in the harsh Outback environment are for sale here, so grab your mates and get shopping!

KIMBARA BULLETIN BOARD

Visit the bulletin board in Kimbara Outback to see the winning entries from the latest National Geographic Kids contests!

Jamaa's wild world of Kimbara Outback is based on a real-life wild place in Australia, the only continent occupied entirely by a single country. The Australian outback is the vast and harsh interior wilderness of this country.

While many call the interior of the Australian continent the outback, this vast area goes by a lot of different names. Australians are more likely to call it the bush, but it's also known as the "back of beyond," "never-never," and "back country."

The land of never-never isn't without civilization! Located in the heart of the outback is the town of Alice Springs. Tucked away in a red desert landscape, this place got its start 140 years ago as a telegraph station. It soon grew into a frontier settlement. Today, this remote town is a bustling tourist destination as people use it as a gateway for exploring the central Australian outback. Alice Springs is also a great place to learn about pioneer history, Aboriginal culture, and to hike and explore mountain ranges, desert parks, and nature trails.

ALPHA TIP

PECK

Every pet in Jamaa does a fun trick when you click on them. Some pets, like hummingbirds and joeys, do different tricks depending on which accessories they have!

238

An Australian dingo patrols the outback.

This farming fence line stretches as far as the eye can see in southern Queensland.

THE RUGGED, RURAL OUTBACK OF Australia is known for being a land crawling with deadly snakes, dangerous crocodiles, and scorching temperatures. Few people live here. Of the more than 23 million people who call Australia home, the majority reside in cities near the coast. The 60,000 people who do live in the outback survive by sheep and cattle ranching and mining. The native people of Australia, the Aboriginals, are nomadic hunters and gatherers.

If you believe the outback habitat consists mostly of dry desert land, you'd be partially right. The outback comprises many deserts. The five largest are the Great Victoria Desert, the Great Sandy Desert, the Tanami Desert, the Simpson Desert, and the Gibson Desert. But this enormous region of Australia is also home to mountain ranges, savannas, grasslands, and woodlands.

More than 15 million years ago, this area was a lush rain forest. But it began drying out, and today it features mostly hot weather and arid soil. Yet this land has a natural beauty. Red sand deserts, rock formations, hot springs, and gorges are just some of the sights people clamor to see when touring here.

The idea of the outback being home to kangaroos is a true one, although kangaroos live in other places in Australia, not just here. The outback is also home to dingoes, a species of wild dog. The largest wild camel population in the world lives here, too! They share the land with snakes, spiders, lizards, and wallabies.

Happy Hopper:
Wallabies are marsupials, or pouched mammals. Their powerful hind legs give them the ability to jump long distances.

THE First AUSTRALIANS

A traditional culture

ABORIGINALS, THE NATIVE PEOPLE OF AUSTRALIA, HAD the continent to themselves for nearly 50,000 years before the establishment of the first European settlement in 1788. They're actually one of the oldest living populations in the world. Today, indigenous people make up only 3 percent of Australia's population.

Australia is a vast continent with many types of climates and terrain. The Aboriginals, who believe in living in harmony with their environment, were able to survive in rain forests, deserts, and everywhere in between. But when European colonization began to take place, many Aboriginals were killed or forced to leave their lands.

Today, Aboriginals still maintain their traditional culture. As a people influenced greatly by the natural world, their art, music, and dance reflect that as well as their spiritual beliefs.

Deadliest Animals of Australia

Saltwater Crocodiles

Salties are what Australians call saltwater crocodiles, the biggest, baddest creatures found in the outback! Salties can be aggressive, territorial, and they are known to attack humans.

Inland Taipans

Meet the most poisonous snakes in the world, inland taipans. One bite from just one of these snakes delivers enough paralyzing venom to kill 100 men! Luckily these snakes rarely bite humans.

Sydney Funnel-Web Spiders

The prize goes to Australia for what is likely the world's most poisonous spider! The venom of Sydney funnel-web spiders is one of the most toxic to humans of all the spider species.

THE MOST LETHAL ANIMALS IN AUSTRALIA—
AND THE WORLD—ARE FOUND NOT IN
THE OUTBACK BUT ON THE COAST NEAR THE
GREAT BARRIER REEF. THE POWERFUL VENOM OF BOX
JELLYFISH CAN KILL IN MINUTES!

Eastern Brown Snakes

Eastern brown snakes are
the second most toxic snake
species in the world, but
they rank first in Australia
for causing the most snake-
bite deaths every year!

Redback Spiders

If you're using the dunny
(bathroom) in the outback,
check under the toilet seat
first! Deadly redback spiders
like to hide there, as well as
in mailboxes and cupboards!

Tiger Snakes

Pretty stripes, deadly venom!
Tiger snakes get their name
because of their tigerlike
stripes. They cause the second highest number of snake
bites in Australia.

SO YOU WANT TO BE A KOALA?

Pouch Escape: When a koala joey leaves Mom's pouch, the baby will ride on her back or cling to her belly!

LET OUT YOUR LOUDEST BELLOW!

YOU CAN'T TELL just by looking at koalas' adorable faces, but these tree dwellers are actually one of nature's loudmouths. Their bellows sound like a combination of an ear-rattling burp and a snore!

Eucalyptus trees provide both food and shelter for these pouched mammals, or marsupials, who spend almost all of their time searching for the tastiest leaves. But eucalyptus leaves are poisonous, tough to digest, and not very nutritious. But koalas' specially adapted digestive system extracts every drop of energy from the leaves while neutralizing their toxins, making the leaves safe to eat and healthy at the same time. Because of their diet, koalas smell a lot like cough drops!

Are You a Koala?

IF YOU'RE OFTEN THE LOUDEST VOICE IS THE ROOM, BUT ALSO LOVE TO NAP, YOU'LL ENJOY BEING A NOISY (YET ADORABLE) KOALA!

STATS

KOALA

- ▸ TYPE: Mammal
- ▸ DIET: Eucalyptus leaves
- ▸ LIFE SPAN: 20 years
- ▸ SIZE: Up to 33 inches (84 cm)
- ▸ WEIGHT: 20 pounds (9 kg)
- ▸ STATUS: Threatened
- ▸ WHERE THEY LIVE: Australia

Red kangaroos are the largest marsupials in the world. But at birth, infants are smaller than a cherry.

Are You a Kangaroo?

IF THIS IS THE ANIMAL FOR YOU, YOU'RE PROBABLY ALWAYS BOUNCING FROM ONE FUN ACTIVITY TO THE NEXT! IT'S FOR JAMMERS WHO ARE UNIQUE AND ATHLETIC.

... or a KANGAROO?

HOP to it!

TODAY, MOST PEOPLE IN THE world are familiar with these hopping marsupials that carry their babies in a pouch on their belly. Kangaroos have very big feet, which enable them to leap 30 feet (9 m) in a single bound! They can also travel at speeds of 30 miles an hour (48 km/h). Their huge tails help to balance them as they leap amazing distances.

The term "kangaroo" broadly refers to a family of more than 60 species, including rat kangaroos and wallabies. Gray kangaroos, red kangaroos, and wallaroos are referred to as the great kangaroos because they are larger than all the other species.

STATS

RED KANGAROO

▸ TYPE: Mammal
▸ DIET: Grass, leaves, and roots
▸ LIFE SPAN: Up to 23 years
▸ SIZE: 6 feet (1.8 m) tall
▸ WEIGHT: 200 pounds (90 kg)
▸ WHERE THEY LIVE: Australia

AUSSIE
WILD WORLD WONDERS

SO OUT OF THIS WORLD, YOU WON'T BELIEVE YOUR EYES!

THE SPECTACULAR "LAND DOWN under" is not only home to a sprawling desert, but it also has some of the most unique natural wonders on Earth. Take a trip over to Middle Island, off the southern coast of western Australia, to find Lake Hillier, which sounds pretty normal—until you realize that its waters are bubblegum pink! The water stays pink even when bottled, and you can even swim in this luminous lake. Scientists think that the bright hue of this 2,000-foot (610-m)-long body of water comes from algae, bacteria, or even salt. And if that's not enough, check out Wave Rock, a 49-foot (15-m)-high granite slab near the town of Hyden that looks like the perfect spot to hang ten. This cool and crazy rock formation is ancient—it's 2.7 billion years old! With so much to discover, it's no wonder that tourists flock to this amazing continent to catch a glimpse of some truly out-of-this-world places.

Wacky Wave: Geologists call Wave Rock's famous formation a "flared slope."

This view of Central Australia's Ayers Rock shows its rich red color.

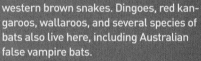

Ayers Rock
A Sacred Stone

FROM A LAND OF FLAT PLAINS rises a majestic, massive rock. Its red color almost makes you believe you've landed on a Martian landscape. Yet the largest monolith, or single stone rock, in the world is located in the middle of the outback!

Ayers Rock, or Uluru as the Aboriginal owners of this landmark call it, can be found in Central Australia in the Uluru-Kata Tjuta National Park. This famous natural attraction rises 1,142 feet (348 m) above the plain and is 2.2 miles (3.6 km) long and 1.2 miles (1.9 km) wide. That's a big rock!

It's not only the size of Ayers Rock that makes it special. Formed more than 500 million years ago, it's made of feldspar-rich sandstone called arkose. The Aboriginals consider it a sacred place where their ancestors originated. They'll guide visitors to the base of the rock during sunrise to see the spectacular changing colors as the rays of the sun play upon it. More than 250,000 people visit Ayers Rock each year.

The national park where Uluru is found is home to more than 150 bird species and reptiles like monitor lizards and western brown snakes. Dingoes, red kangaroos, wallaroos, and several species of bats also live here, including Australian false vampire bats.

The next time you visit Kimbara Outback, head over to the wooden deck and check out the view. The big rock in the distance bears a striking resemblance to Uluru!

A lace monitor lizard looks out over the desert in Australia's Mungo National Park.

Aussie WILDLIFE

FILLED WITH UNIQUE CREATURES!

AUSTRALIA IS HOME TO SOME COOL WILDLIFE. THAT'S because this continent, surrounded by both the Pacific and Indian Oceans, is very much isolated from the rest of the world. More than 80 percent of the mammals, reptiles, plants, and frogs here can be found nowhere else on the planet! If any of these animals were to disappear from Australia, they'd be extinct on Earth.

Today, 86 Australian animal species are considered critically endangered, which is the highest risk of extinction. Some of the species are small marsupials like Gilbert's potoroo, woylies, and Kangaroo Island dunnarts.

Tasmanian devils, feisty mammals famous for their scary growls, were almost wiped out as pests by farmers until they were made a protected species in 1941. They made a comeback, but a contagious illness wiped out huge numbers of the devils. Scientists are working on a cure to save this species from extinction.

Tasmanian devil

Wacky Aussie Animals!

Check out more of the weird but amazing creatures that call the land down under home.

Quokkas

These merry marsupials hang out in groups, called clans, and spend their days dining on swamp peppermint, hopping around like kangaroos, and digging tunnels to hide and nap in.

Duck-Billed Platypuses

Platypuses have otter-like furry bodies, duck-like bills, webbed feet, and wide beaver-like tails. If that wasn't enough, they also have pointy spurs that are poisonous!

Wild Cassowaries

These giant flightless birds are taller than adult humans. With their daggerlike claws—watch out!— they're considered the world's most dangerous bird.

Short-Beaked Echidnas

Echidnas are monotremes—mammals that lay eggs. Stranger still, these creatures find food by a process called electrolocation, meaning they use electrical signals to locate their prey.

Dingoes

These wild Australian dogs likely arrived between 3,000 and 4,000 years ago aboard ships from Asia. Today, the continent is home to so many dingoes they're considered pests.

DESTINATION A.J.

GABBY'S ANIMAL HOSPITAL

G'day, mate! Within the sun-soaked wilds of Kimbara Outback, you'll find Gabby's Animal Hospital. Gabby Wild is a veterinarian and wildlife conservationist, which means that she's passionate about keeping animals healthy and safe. At the hospital, Gabby gives medical care to all kinds of animals, including her horse buddy, Bu. You can even watch tons of fun videos of Gabby answering Jammers' questions and interacting with animals in the wild.

You can always pop in anytime to learn about some of the tools Gabby uses to examine and treat her patients, and buy bandages, braces, casts, and stethoscopes at the Hospital Shop. Come see for yourself how happy animals are in their natural habitats, and why the environment and the creatures within it are worth our protection.

Outstanding Outback!

HOW MUCH DO YOU KNOW ABOUT THE AMAZING LAND DOWN UNDER? QUIZ YOURSELF AND FIND OUT!

#1 Wallabies' powerful hind legs give them the ability to:

a. skip on hot sand
b. jump long distances
c. dive deep underwater
d. kick predators

#2 Rains during the rainy season bring more water to northern Australia than London sees in a year.
True or False?

#3 Native people in Australia believe that frogs are a good luck charm that help plants grow.
True or False?

#4 Kangaroos lick their ears to stay cool.
True or False?

#5 Crickets detect sounds through which body part?

a. stomach
b. eyes
c. knees
d. mouth

#6 Where do koalas get the water they need?

a. in the Tasman Sea
b. in the leaves they eat
c. from rivers and streams
d. from hoses in people's gardens

#7 One of the most lethal animals in the world lives off the coast of Australia. What is it?

a. sea turtle
b. pufferfish
c. box jellyfish
d. moray eel

#8 What percentage of Australia's animals can be found nowhere else on the planet?

a. 30%
b. 80%
c. 35%
d. 70%

#9 Male platypuses can sting other animals with poisonous barbs on their _____.

a. hind legs
b. tongues
c. tails
d. bellies

#10 Most camels live in Africa, Asia, and Australia. What are baby camels called?

a. calves
b. pups
c. kids
d. foals

#11 What are baby koalas called?

a. cubs
b. kids
c. joeys
d. kittens

#12 What is the giant rock formation in the outback?

a. the Grand Canyon
b. Easter Island
c. Ayers Rock
d. Stonehenge

#13 Tasmanian devils, marsupials found only on the Australian island of Tasmania, are about the size of which of the following when they're born?

a. a raisin
b. a golf ball
c. an ice-cream sandwich
d. a box of breakfast cereal

SPOT ON!

LOOK FOR THIS GREAT GAME
IN KIMBARA OUTBACK

Find the answers on page 265.

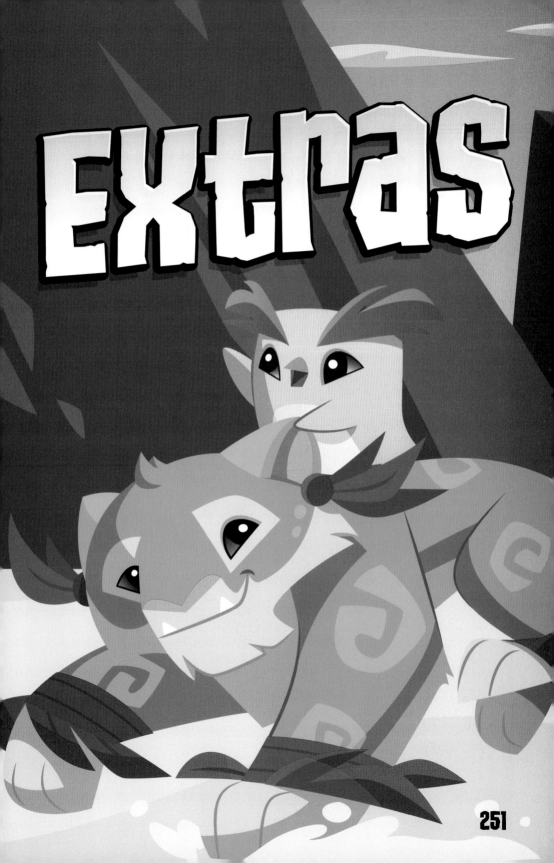

THE MAKING OF ANIMAL JAM

Take a Peek Behind the Scenes!

HAVE YOU EVER WONDERED HOW YOUR favorite AJ animal, place, or game was created? Take a rare look behind the scenes of Animal Jam and learn from the pros at WildWorks, the studio that brings the characters to life on your computer screen!

It takes more than a village to create the world of Jamaa. It's more like an army of animators, character designers, environment designers, illustrators, 3-D modelers, writers, game designers, and musicians are all needed to bring Jamaa to life. Programmers and Web designers help turn their creations into the animals and worlds you visit and play with every day!

The Origin of the Alphas and Pets

AFTER CREATING THE ANIMALS, THE NEXT big challenge for the art team was designing the Alphas. The artists drew upon movies from their childhoods—like *Thundercats, Goonies, The Lion King, The Muppets, The Secret of NIMH,* and *Star Wars*—for inspiration. When drawing the Alphas, WildWorks artists make sure their poses are strong to highlight their epicness!

Pets, on the other hand, should be the most adorable creatures you've ever seen. The art team likens pets to marshmallows injected with sweet frosting, sprinkled with sugar. If a new pet doesn't make players squee or cry a little with joy, it's not cute enough! WildWorks artists use the most basic shapes for creating pets, called the "baby formula": a colossal head with almost no body. They must be smaller than the smallest Animal Jam animal.

Animal Art: Every Animal Jam animal goes through many rounds of sketches. Here are some you may recognize!

Animal Jam Artist Q&A

Here's how the original animals were created, according to the WildWorks art team:

Creating the Animals

When the art team first started on the original sketches for the initial Animal Jam animals, they were too cute. After an extensive review, the designers knew they needed to make them look older, more like teenagers. That's when the style that players see today started to emerge. The artists decided to mute the colors and to make the animals' heads smaller. Square shapes and counter curves are the basic structure of each animal—scaly skin or fur is then added. Every animal is meant to resemble a great toy that you would want to own and display somewhere.

Making the Cut

Among the first animals the art team created were a pig and a dinosaur! Why didn't they make it into Jamaa? WildWorks took a poll of *National Geographic Kids* readers and asked them to pick their favorites. It was up to the players. Even now, the new animals Wild-Works put in the game come from player feedback. So don't rule out snakes or even dinosaurs in Jamaa just yet!

The Horrid Wasteland of Frumpy Things

The bottom line: If an animal is not cool or cute or both, it does not belong in Animal Jam! But rejected designs and ideas don't just disappear. The art team keeps them all in a special place, which they jokingly call "The Horrid Wasteland of Frumpy Things"!

BUILDING JAMAA

CREATING THE COOLEST WORLDS!

THE SUNNY SHORES OF CRYSTAL Sands, the dark Sarepia Forest, the towering heights of Mt. Shiveer. These worlds didn't exist until the WildWorks team created them. Now all Jammers can splash in the waves at Crystal Sands, climb the tallest trees in Sarepia Forest, and trek up snowy Mt. Shiveer.

New lands are added to Jamaa from time to time. What's next? Keep playing wild to find out!

How are worlds created? Environment designers draw their inspiration from real-life biomes around the world. A few sketches kick-start the brainstorming, and once an idea is fully formed, it's full steam ahead! Yet even when the finished land makes its debut in Jamaa, it's still not quite done. You, the players, bring it to life by exploring and playing wild in it!

How'd They Do That?

IT'S ONE THING TO HAVE AN IDEA FOR A GREAT ANIMAL CHARACTER OR AN AWESOME new world. But how does it get from an artist's imagination to your computer screen? Technology! The team at WildWorks uses software programs like Adobe Photoshop, Illustrator, and Flash, as well as Autodesk Maya 3-D Animation, to create the virtual characters and lands you know so well. Over 3,000 pictures are drawn to complete just one animal. The process takes about two and a half months.

Bringing a new land to Jamaa can take from six weeks to two months. The design team builds upon the rough sketches of the environment. Once the new land is finished, they begin to test it for any bugs or glitches. They also get to play in the new land to make sure it's a fun one, where Jammers will have a blast!

The Beginnings of Jamaa

WHERE'S THE BEST PLACE TO PLAY WILD?
In a jungle, of course!

When WildWorks environment designers first began to create the world of Jamaa, they needed a main place for players to land when entering the game. To capture the adventure of Jamaa, they decided on a jungle theme. In the initial concept sketches, trees were heavily featured. The designers studied rain forests around the world. They were especially inspired by Angkor Wat, an ancient city built in the tropical rain forest of Cambodia over 800 years ago. The concept changed, and ancient ruins and statues sprung up among the trees. Jamaa's Lost Temple of Zios was born!

You might be thinking that Jamaa Township, not the Lost Temple of Zios, is the central hub of Jamaa and the first place new players enter. And you're right! The design process is always changing and one idea can lead to another.

After the Lost Temple of Zios was created, the designers went to work on Jamaa Township. Their goal: create a land that looked like the animals themselves had built it. The buildings would be primitive, chunky, and more crudely assembled than you'd see in a modern, human city. No synthetic materials, like plastic, metal, or vinyl, would be used.

The finished design captured a welcoming village center with inviting storefronts—and prompted the decision to make Jamaa Township the central point from which players would embark on their adventures. After a quick tutorial, all new Jammers are dropped off in Jamaa Township.

As the designers add new lands, they always strive to meet their key objective: to create exciting places where Jammers can explore and experience awesome adventures!

Building Environments: Many drafts came before the final look for the Lost Temple of Zios was achieved.

GAMES IN JAMAA

Games are a great way to earn Gems, play with buddies, or just have some fun!

DISC TOSS!

Ever wonder what life is like for a pet puppy? Play this game to find out. Catch as many flying discs as you can—the faster they fly, the faster you'll need to chase them!

BEST DRESSED

Play dress-up for a chance to win Gems in Best Dressed! Choose the colors and wardrobe you think best match the theme and strut your stuff on the stage. If other Jammers like your look, they'll vote for you. If you get a lot of votes, you can win lots of Gems! Find this game in Coral Canyons. There's even an ocean version especially for ocean animals in Bahari Bay.

Brady Barr's CHEMISTRY SET

Have you always wanted a chemistry set to experiment with? Dr. Brady Barr will let you borrow his anytime you want. Just stop by his lab in the Lost Temple of Zios.

THE CLAW

For the cost of five Gems, you can try your luck at winning a plushie from one of the many claw machines located around Jamaa, including in Appondale, Sarepia Forest, and Crystal Sands.

DOUBLE UP

The animals are hiding in their holes. Can you find them by matching up pairs of tigers, bunnies, pandas, and birds? Go to Crystal Sands to start making animal matches.

DUCKY DASH

Help your pet ducky outrun the waterfall! Don't get stunned by leaping frogs or stuck behind floating sticks or lily pads. As you go, collect rubber duckies along the way for Gems—golden duckies are worth even more!

Food Games

Throughout Jamaa are places where you can make a snack for yourself. Grab some buttery popcorn at the **POPCORN MACHINE**, a warm cup of cocoa at the **HOT COCOA MACHINE**, or a refreshing smoothie at the **SMOOTHIE MACHINE**.

Nom nom nom! Find out what it's like to be part of the ocean food chain in this eat-or-be-eaten game. Feast on smaller fish but avoid the bigger fish who'd like to make a meal out of you. Dive into Crystal Reef to start chomping.

It's dinnertime and a bunch of hungry animals have come to you for help. Dish up the correct orders as quickly as you can, but be careful to give each customer exactly what they ask for! Play this delicious game in Crystal Sands.

In this pinball-like game, you shoot balls. Depending on where your ball lands, you'll earn Gems. Try to shoot the ball into the face of Zios. It will light up. If you light up all three suns you'll earn a Gem bonus! This game can be found in the Chamber of Knowledge in the Lost Temple of Zios.

The sky is falling! Actually, it's even worse than that. Nasty Phantoms are erupting from a volcano, and it's up to you and five other Jammers to avoid the falling Phantoms and last as long as you can without being hit by one. The last Jammer standing wins! Start running for cover in the Lost Temple of Zios.

The Phantoms are hiding out in forts, and it's up to you, your trusty slingshot, and some fruit to save the day! Once you destroy all the Phantoms in a fort you move on to the next level. Different types of fruit can do different damage to the forts and the Phantoms, so pay attention. Go to Appondale to start flinging fruit.

Match Gems to knock them down and to clear Phantoms who are trapped in the ice. If you break five or more Gems you'll create a combo and earn bonus points! This icy game is in Mt. Shiveer.

Make a moat around your sand castle in Overflow! Connect the paths to your castle so the water will flow. The longer the path, the more Gems you will earn. Have fun digging in the sand at Crystal Sands.

Meet the hungry, hungry hedgehog! He needs to gobble up as many berries as he can. Guide him through the maze, but watch out for those pesky Phantoms. If the hedgehog gobbles up a special crystal, he can turn the table on the Phantoms and catch them. Head over to Sarepia Forest to start playing.

How far can an armadillo go? Find out in Long Shot! Fling the armadillo as far as you can to earn Gems. If you land your armadillo on geysers or moles, you'll get an extra burst of speed that will take it even farther. This game is in Coral Canyons.

A swarm of angry insects is headed your way. The only way to stop them is to strategically place animals that love to eat bugs—like snakes, frogs, and lizards—in their path. If you let an insect escape, your health will be damaged. Bring on the bug control in Appondale.

And they're off! Race to the finish line against five other Jammers in this fast-paced game. But watch out for any obstacles in your way. You'll need to jump over them in order to stay in the lead. If you have a horse, you'll automatically play as that when you go into the game. If not, one will be provided for you. Start your day at the races in Jamaa Township.

What Mira says goes! Watch the pattern of colors and sounds, then try to copy them. The more you match, the longer (and harder!) the pattern gets. The faster you duplicate the pattern, the more Gems you will earn. Test your copying skills in the Chamber of Knowledge in the Lost Temple of Zios.

Wash your pet in Crystal Sands! Spray, scrub, and soap your pet until it's sparkling clean!

In this game, which can be found in Sol Arcade in Jamaa Township, you have just one shot to take down the Phantom ship. If you win, you'll get a cool toy for your den! It costs 10 Gems to play this game.

Shoot pill bugs from a tulip to clear the screen of ladybugs and earn Gems. Each time you clear a level you'll learn a fun fact about pill bugs. If you have any leftover pill bugs you'll score a bonus! Bug out over this game in Sarepia Forest.

Evil Phantoms are flying high above Jamaa and threatening this land's peaceful existence! Grab a spaceship to stop them. The tricky red Phantoms will need to be hit more than once to defeat them. Play Phantom Fighter in Jamaa Township.

Search for the hidden treasures in the picture. The faster you find them, the more Gems you'll get. If you get stuck, use a hint. But if you can figure out where the treasure is hiding without using hints, you'll get a bonus! Swim to the very bottom of Deep Blue to start your treasure hunt.

Located at the top of Coral Canyons is one of the most popular games in Jamaa: Sky High. Bounce off the clouds and soar through the air as you collect Gems. If you can bounce your way to the very top and reach the treasure chest, you'll win a special rare item!

 **Sssssnake!**

Play as your pet snake and catch as many mice as you can! For every mouse you eat, your body grows longer and longer and you slither faster and faster ... Watch out! If you run into your own tail, you're out!

Test your skills in Bahari Bay as you race your dolphin to the finish line. Be sure to avoid all obstacles or you'll slow down. If you have a dolphin, you'll play as that. If not, you'll get a loaner dolphin for the duration of the race.

Recycling is a supercool thing to do. When you do it in Sarepia Forest while playing Super Sort, you can even earn Gems! Sort the items into their correct recycling bins. If you sort them all without making a mistake you'll get a Gem bonus!

Spiders have invaded the trees of Jamaa. Help stop them by zapping spiders in Jamaa Township. Zapping more spiders earns you more Gems. Zap every spider in a round to earn a Gem bonus!

How much do you know about mammals, reptiles, amphibians, birds, bugs, or marine life? Pick from one of these five categories, then click on the screen. Slowly an animal will be revealed—guess what it is before time runs out. The faster you do the more Gems you win! This game can be found in Kimbara Outback.

Head to the eagle's nest in Coral Canyons to play Swoopy Eagle! Use your mouse or the space bar to flap your wings and soar through the cacti. Just be careful not to touch any part of the cacti—especially the spines!

ALPHA TIP

Feeling festive? In both Animal Jam and Play Wild!, new games are released for a limited time at certain times during the year

PECK

Calling all smarties! Put your knowledge about animals and our planet to the test by playing a round of the challenging Temple of Trivia in the Lost Temple of Zios. Compete against other Jammers by answering the multiple-choice questions. The quicker you answer, the more Gems you'll win!

When you visit Tierney's Aquarium in Crystal Sands, you can discover exotic marine animals, learn facts, and win awesome prizes! Touch different creatures long enough to fill the timer. Fill your Touch Pool log to earn cool prizes.

Located on the Canyons Pathway that connects Coral Canyons to Crystal Sands, Twister is a game where you help a bird escape a tornado! Avoid buildings and flying debris to escape the twister. Fly through the rings to get a score bonus.

Take a relaxing parachute ride down to the ground as you collect Gems. Wait—we forgot to mention the Phantoms! They'll get in your way and try to take your Gems from you. If you can reach the ground without hitting a Phantom you'll get a Gem bonus! Climb to the top of the trees in Sarepia Forest to play this game.

Play Wild! Games

There are even more amazing mini games exclusive to the mobile version of Animal Jam. Play them all!

SINGLE PLAYER
A Puppy's Tale
Block Break
Escape The Phantoms
Jumbled Up
Phantom Dodger
Roll!!!!!

BUDDY GAMES
Checkers
King Pin
Ladybug Lane
Pop'n
Super Cube
Trivia

ANSWER KEY

Pages 88–89
Jamaa Township

Pages 104–105
Lost Temple of Zios

Pages 124–125
Appondale

1) D. 2) False. Giraffes lie down to sleep. 3) D. 4) A. 5) False. In East Africa, some male lions do not have manes. 6) C. 7) True. Although a zebra's teeth grow throughout its entire life, grazing and chewing wears them down. 8) A. 9) A. 10) D. 11) False. A rhinoceros's horn grows from its skin. 12) D.

Pages 142–143
Sarepia Forest

Pages 160–161
Coral Canyons

1) False. They can dive as fast as 200 miles an hour (161 km/h). 2) C. 3) D. 4) D. 5) A. 6) A. 7) D. 8) A. 9) B. 10) True. This is due to the tilt of the Earth's axis. And in the winter at the poles, the sun never rises! 11) False. The Gobi desert is a cold desert with occasional snow on its dunes.

Pages 174–175
Crystal Sands

Pages 184–185
Bahari Bay

Pages 196–197
Crystal Reef

Pages 208–209
Kani Cove

INDEX BOLDFACE INDICATES ILLUSTRATIONS

ILLUSTRATION CREDITS

AL: Alamy; DRT: Dreamstime; GI: Getty Images; NGC: National Geographic Creative; NPL: Nature Picture Library; SS: Shutterstock

32 (LO CTR LE), Jason Kasumovic/SS; 32 (LO LE), Janelle Lugge/SS; 32 (LO CTR RT), edella/SS; 38 (UP), Gnel Karapetyan/DRT; 39 (UP LE), Fabrice Coffrini/AFP/GI; 39 (UP RT), Manjunath Kiran/EPA/Newscom; 39 (CTR LE), Marvin Joseph/The Washington Post via GI; 39 (CTR RT), ullstein bild/ullstein bild via GI; 39 (LO CTR), Granger, NYC—All rights reserved; 49 (UP LE), Photo by Hulton-Deutsch Collection/Corbis/Corbis via GI; 49 (CTR RT), Photo by George Rinhart/Corbis via GI; 49 (LO LE), NASA; 49 (LO LE), Brady Barr; 49 (LO CTR), Mike Johnson/NGC; 49 (LO RT), Gabby Wild; 51 (UP), Courtesy of Gary A. Rohde; 51 (UP CTR), Ed Jones/AFP/GI; 51 (LO CTR), AP Photo/Cecil Whig, Adelma Gregory-Bunnel; 51 (LO), Joanne Lefson; 53 (UP RT), NAS/Photo Researchers/GI; 53 (CTR RT), Hulton Archive/GI; 53 (CTR LE), sittipong/SS; 57 (UP RT), Volodymyr Byrdyak/DRT; 57 (UP LE), Mgkuijpers/DRT; 57 (LO RT), Juniors Bildarchiv GmbH/AL; 57 (LO LE), Alanjeffery/DRT; 58 (LE), Johan W. Elzenga/SS; 58 (CTR), rashworth/SS; 58 (RT), Maslov Dmitry/SS; 61 (UP), Brown/GTphoto; 61 (CTR RT), Karine Aigner/NG Staff; 61 (LO LE), Noah Goodrich/Caters News; 63, Andresr/SS; 66, Ksenia Raykova/SS; 69 (UP), Reuters/Thomas Peter Odly; 69 (CTR), Donna Kassewitz/SpeakDolphin; 69 (LO), Dean Pomerleau; 73 (UP), Juniors Bildarchiv GmbH/AL; 73 (CTR RT), Mark Moffett/Minden Pictures; 73 (LO), Phil Crosby/AL; 76-77 (BACK), IR Stone/SS; 76 (UP), leungchopan/SS; 76 (LO CTR RT), Kwiktor/DRT; 76 (LO RT), David Coleman/DRT; 77 (UP LE), Roberto Marinello/DRT; 77 (UP RT), Simon Hack/DRT; 77 (LO), Typhoonski/DRT; 78-79, Zaramira/DRT; 78 (LO), Juhku/SS; 80 (UP), Justpeachy/DRT; 80 (LO), Rob Hyrons/SS; 81, Vasilyev Alexandr/SS; 82, Scattoselvaggio/DRT; 83, Nyker1/DRT; 84-85 (BACK), Borna Mirahmadian/SS; 85 (UP LE), Mike Clarke/AFP/GI; 85 (UP RT), Tim Flach/GI; 85 (CTR LE), ROX/rox.co.uk; 85 (CTR RT), CB2/ZOB/WENN/Newscom; 85 (LO LE), Joffet Emmanuel/Sipa; 86, talseN/SS; 87, Johner Images/AL Stock Photo; 88-89, Sergei Kazakov/SS; 92 (CTR RT), Dr. Morley Read/SS; 92 (CTR), Robyn Mackenzie/SS; 92 (LO LE), Brady Barr; 93 (UP LE), Robert Clark/NGC; 93 (UP RT), incamerastock/AL; 93 (LO), Peter Adams Photography Ltd/AL; 94-95, Aditya Singh/GI; 94 (UP), Don Johnston/GI; 95 (LO RT), Nick Biemans/SS; 96-97 (BACK), jarnbeer19/SS; 97 (UP LE), holbox/SS; 97 (UP RT), f9photos/SS; 97 (LO), Vadim Petrakov/SS; 98, Vilainecrevette/SS; 99, Scanrail1/SS; 100-101 (BACK), 009fotofriends/SS; 100 (CTR), Edurivero/DRT; 100 (LO LE), Palko72/DRT; 101 (CTR LE), Anton_Ivanov/SS; 101 (LO LE), Dirk Ercken/DRT; 101 (LO RT), Anton_Ivanov/SS; 102 (BACK), szefei/SS; 102 (UP), Morley Read/DRT; 102 (CTR LE), Kjersti Joergensen/DRT; 102 (CTR LE), Dirk Ercken/SS; 102 (LO), Larry Larsen/AL; 103 (CTR), Roland Seitre/NPL; 108 (BACK), Taiga/SS; 108 (UP), Ekawrecker/DRT; 108 (CTR RT), Frans Lanting/NGC; 109 (BACK), Donald Sawvel/SS; 109 (UP LE), Ajn/DRT; 109 (UP RT), Ramblingman/DRT; 109 (LO), Ariadne Van Zandbergen/AL; 110-111, Suzi Eszterhas/NPL; 111 (LO), Peter Blackwell/NPL; 112 (BACK), piotr_pabijan/SS; 112 (UP CTR), Isselee/DRT; 112 (CTR RT), Peter Wollinga/DRT;

112 (LO LE), Beverly Joubert/NGC; 113 (CTR), Nico Smit/DRT; 114, Frans Lanting/NGC; 115, Tony Heald/NPL; 116, Byelikova/DRT; 117, Tudorish/DRT; 117 (CTR LE), Andries Alberts/DRT; 118-119, Maximilian Weinzierl/AL; 119 (CTR RT), Brady Barr; 119 (LO), Frans Lanting/Mint Images/Biosphoto; 120 (UP), Aurora Photos/AL; 120 (LO), David Woodfall/NPL; 121 (LO), Jouan & Rius/NPL; 121 (UP), Jim Parkin/AL; 122, Papa Bravo/SS; 123, kungverylucky/SS; 124 (UP), Dzain/DRT; 124 (CTR RT), William Davies/iStockphoto; 124 (LO), Angelika Stern/iStockphoto; 125 (UP), Emanuelataurino/DRT; 125 (LE), Angelika Stern/DRT; 128-129 (BACK), pani/SS; 128 (UP), un.bolovan/SS; 128 (CTR RT), BMJ/SS; 129 (UP LE), Phil Schermeister/NGC; 129 (UP RT), Jordan Siemens/GI; 129 (LO), Tom Reichner/SS; 130 (UP LE), Jim and Jamie Dutcher/NGC; 131 (UP), Jim Cumming/GI; 131 (LO), Jim and Jamie Dutcher/NGC; 132-133, Tischenko Irina/SS; 133 (UP RT), Francisco Javier Gil Oreja/DRT; 133 (UP CTR), Matt Freedman/DanitaDelimont/Newscom; 133 (LO CTR), age fotostock/AL; 133 (LO RT), Robin Weaver/AL; 134, Tom Reichner/SS; 135, Gerald A. DeBoer/SS; 136 (UP), Christian Ziegler/Minden Pictures; 136 (LO), quebecfoto/AL; 137 (UP), Don Mammoser/SS; 137 (LO), Brian J Skerry/NGC; 138, Dndavis/DRT; 139, Dean Bertoncelj/SS; 140-141, Neale Clark/robertharding/AL; 141 (CTR RT), P.Burghardt/SS; 142-143, Rebecca Hale/NG Staff; 146 (CTR), Danita Delimont/AL; 146 (LO RT), Americanspirit/DRT; 146 (LO CTR), William Michael Norton/DRT; 147 (LO LE), Mike P Shepherd/AL; 147 (UP RT), apdesign/SS; 147 (UP LE), Michael Elliott/DRT; 148, Colin Harris/era-images/AL; 149, Shchipkova Elena/SS; 150, totajla/SS; 151, Pim Leijen/SS; 152-153 (BACK), Horizon International Images Limited/AL; 153 (UP LE), Karenwinton/DRT; 153 (UP RT), Aurora Photos/AL; 154, Chris Hill/SS; 155, Derek R. Audette/SS; 156 (BACK), Miloslav Doubrava/DRT; 156 (UP LE), Michael D. Kern/NPL/Minden Pictures; 156 (UP CTR), Graham Hatherley/NPL; 156 (LO CTR), Luiz Claudio Marigo/NPL; 156 (LO), Sunheyy/DRT; 157 (LO LE), John Burcham/NGC; 158, Volodymyr Burdiak/SS; 159, Maria Itina/DRT; 160 (UP), Jim Parkin/SS; 160 (LO LE), Evgeniy Baranov/DRT; 161 (UP), Pär Edlund/DRT; 161 (CTR), AngelaLouwe/SS; 161 (LO), Michael Shake/SS; 164-165 (BACK), Ron Dale/SS; 164 (UP CTR), Stephen Frink Collection/AL; 164 (UP RT), Steve Hull Photography/SS; 164 (LO CTR), Sandra Van Der Steen/DRT; 165 (UP), Oleg Znamenskiy/DRT; 165 (CTR), Juniors Bildarchiv GmbH/AL; 166, Ioana Grecu/DRT; 167, Shannon Hibberd/NGC; 168-169 (BACK), Ana Del Castillo/DRT; 168 (CTR RT), Konstantin Kulikov/AL; 169 (beach hoppers), Kim Taylor/NPL; 169 (coquina clam), Harry Rogers/GI; 169 (bloodworm), Thomas Ames Jr./Visuals Unlimited, Inc./GI; 169 (sand crab), Chris Gotz/SS; 169 (water bear), Sebastian Kaulitzki/SS; 170-171 (BACK), bikeriderlondon/SS; 171 (UP), Simon Gurney/DRT; 171 (LO), Ian Wilson/DRT; 172-173, Moose Henderson/DRT; 173 (UP), Sylvain Cordier/GI; 173 (LO), Wayne Lynch/GI; 178-179 (BACK), Sundari/SS; 178 (UP), Rudmer Zwerver/SS; 178 (CTR RT), Ahmad FaizaL Yahya/SS; 179 (UP LE), Mechanik/SS; 179 (UP RT), Win Initiative/GI; 179 (LO), SW_Stock/SS; 180, Gomez David/iStockphoto; 181, Salparadis/SS; 182-183 (BACK), Markus Fleute/GI; 183 (UP LE), wim claes/SS; 183 (UP R-T), kropic1/SS; 183 (LO), kropic1/SS; 184-185, Digitally composed artwork by Damien Vignaux; 188-189 (BACK), Klara Viskova/SS; 188 (UP), KKG Photo/SS; 188 (CTR), Predrag Vuckovic/GI; 189 (UP LE), Predrag Vuckovic/GI;

189 (UP RT), Martin Maun/DRT; 190-191 (BACK), Irochka/DRT; 190 (LE), Jamiegodson/DRT; 191 (pygmy seahorse), Song Heming/DRT; 191 (moray eel), Deborah Coles/DRT; 191 (parrotfish), Amilevin/DRT; 191 (sea snake), Mauricio Handler/NGC; 191 (nudibranch), Howard Chew/DRT; 191 (coral gobies), Images & Stories/AL Stock Photo; 192-193, Richard Carey/DRT; 193 (CTR), Jason Edwards/NGC; 194-195 (BACK), Michael Patrick O'Neill/AL; 194 (CTR), Mark Webster/Lonely Planet Images/GI; 195 (UP LE), Michael Patrick O'Neill/AL; 195 (UP RT), Alex Mustard/NPL; 195 (LO), Craig Ruaux/AL; 196-197, Constantinos Petrinos/NPL; 200-201 (BACK), Goldenarts/SS; 200 (UP CTR LE), Olga Khoroshunova/DRT; 200 (UP RT), Liquid Productions, LLC/SS; 200 (CTR RT), Ofer Ketter/SeaPics.com; 200 (LO LE), Jeff Rotman/AL; 201 (UP LE), Emory Kristof/NGC; 201 (UP RT), Emory Kristof/NGC; 201 (LO RT), Bruce Dale/NGC; 201 (LO CTR), Interfoto/AL Stock Photo; 202-203 (BACK), Sergey Dubrov/SS; 202 (LO LE), Sisse Brimberg/NGC; 202 (LO CTR), EPA/Cardiff University/Newscom; 202 (LO RT), OME/Polaris/Newscom; 203 (UP RT), Lebrecht Music and Arts Photo Library/AL; 203 (LO CTR), Ray Fairall/Zuma Press; 203 (LO LE), Jonathan Nackstrand/AFP/GI; 203 (CTR LE), VCG Wilson/Corbis via GI; 204-205, Luis Javier Sandoval/GI; 205 (UP RT), Masa Ushioda/SeaPics.com; 205 (CTR RT), Stephen Frink/GI; 206-207, Alvov/SS; 207 (UP RT), Hugoht/DRT; 208-209, Digitally composed artwork by Damien Vignaux; 212-213 (BACK), Klara Viskova/SS; 212 (UP RT), Jeff Rotman/AL; 212 (LO LE), Richard Carey/DRT; 213 (UP CTR), Napat/SS; 213 (UP RT), Jurgen Freund/NPL; 214-215, Martin Strmiska/AL; 214 (LO RT), Planctonvideo/DRT; 215 (LO RT), Sue Daly/NPL; 216, David Shale/NPL; 216 (LO RT), David Shale/NPL; 217 (UP LE), NOAA; 217 (UP RT), Dr. Ken MacDonald/Science Source; 217 (LO RT), Doc White/NPL; 217 (LO CTR), Amanda Cotton/AL; 217 (LO LE), David Shale/NPL;218 (LE), Caters News Agency; 218 (LO), Susan Dabritz/SeaPics.com; 219 (UP), Wong Hock weng/SS; 219 (LO), bluehand/SS; 222-223 (BACK), Malchev/SS; 222 (UP), Martin Harvey/AL; 222 (CTR LE), Kodym/DRT; 222 (CTR RT), Mircea Costina/DRT; 222 (LO RT), Lukas Blazek/DRT.; 223 (UP LE), Leo & Mandy Dickinson/NPL; 223 (UP RT), Andy Bardon/NGC; 223 (LO LE), Everett Collection Inc/AL; 224-225, Robert Palmer/SS; 224 (UP LE), Ron Niebrugge/AL; 226-227 (BACK), Old Apple/SS; 226 (LO LE), Rinus Baak/DRT; 226 (LO CTR LE), Robert Preston Photography/AL; 226 (LO CTR RT), Anibal Trejo/DRT; 226 (LO RT), Erika J Mitchell/SS; 228-229, imagebroker/AL; 228 (LO LE), Pete Ryan/NGC; 230-231 (BACK), Dchauy/SS; 231 (UP LE), Eric Baccega/NPL; 231 (UP RT), BMJ/SS; 231 (LO RT), Eric Baccega/NPL; 232, Erni/SS; 233, Daniel J. Cox/GI; 234-235, Rebecca Hale/NG Staff; 238-239 (BACK), Seita/Shuttersock; 238 (UP CTR), Itobiwan/DRT; 238 (CTR RT), David Wall/AL; 239 (UP LE), John Carnemolla/SS; 239 (UP RT), Travelling-light/DRT; 239 (LO RT), Ben Mcleish/DRT; 240-241 (BACK), Wildlight Photo Agency/AL; 240 (LO LE), Brandon Cole Marine Photography/AL; 240 (LO CTR), Robert Valentic/NPL; 240 (LO RT), Roland Seitre/NPL; 241 (LO LE), Robert Valentic/NPL; 241 (LO CTR), Graphic Science/AL; 241 (LO RT), Robert Valentic/NPL; 242, Andras Deak/DRT; 243, imagebroker/AL; 244-245 (BACK), Col Roberts/GI; 244 (LO), Suzanne and Nick Geary/GI; 245 (UP CTR), imagebroker/AL; 245 (LO RT), blickwinkel/AL; 246-247 (BACK), Roland Seitre/NPL; 247 (UP RT), Kevin Schafer/GI; 247 (UP LE), D. Parer and E. Parer-Cook/Minden Pictures; 247 (CTR RT), Lukas Blazek/DRT; 247 (CTR LE), Kristian Bell/SS; 247 (LO RT), Auscape/GI; 248 (RT), Eric Isselee/SS; 248 (CTR), Anatolich/SS; 248 (LO), halimqd/SS; 249 (UP), Andrea Willmore/SS; 249 (CTR RT), D. Parer and E. Parer-Cook/Minden Pictures; 249 (LO), Johncarnemolla/DRT

Since 1888, the National Geographic Society has funded more than 12,000 research, exploration, and preservation projects around the world. The Society receives funds from National Geographic Partners, LLC, funded in part by your purchase. A portion of the proceeds from this book supports this vital work. To learn more, visit natgeo.com/info.

For more information, visit nationalgeographic.com, call 1-800-647-5463, or write to the following address:
    National Geographic Partners
    1145 17th Street N.W.
    Washington, D.C. 20036-4688 U.S.A.

Visit us online at nationalgeographic.com/books

For librarians and teachers: ngchildrensbooks.org

More for kids from National Geographic:
kids.nationalgeographic.com

For information about special discounts for bulk purchases, please contact National Geographic Books Special Sales: specialsales@natgeo.com

For rights or permissions inquiries, please contact National Geographic Books Subsidiary Rights: bookrights@natgeo.com

Designed by Chad Tomlinson
Text contributed by Girl Friday Productions

Trade paperback ISBN: 978-1-4263-2875-6
Reinforced library binding ISBN: 978-1-4263-2876-3

Printed in the United States of America
17/QGT-QGL/1

BRING YOUR JAMMIN' JAMAA ADVENTURES TO LIFE!

Have a great game tip, den design, or habitat tidbit you want to remember? How about cool travel experiences or fun with your friends? This bright, write-in journal is the perfect place to jot down anything that's on your mind—both in and out of the game.

NATIONAL GEOGRAPHIC KiDS

Animal Jam

JOURNAL

Get ready to write wild!

Stretch out those **writing paws** and pick up your **favorite pen**, because this is the ultimate book about Jamaa **created by YOU!** This journal has tons of space for you to write about **anything and everything**—from what you did yesterday after school to a time you saw a wild animal in your backyard. You could even write about what you had for breakfast! **The possibilities are endless.**

In this journal, you can also take the fun of Animal Jam to the next level.

Write a story about a lion, an ow... a flamingo exploring Sarepia Fores... imagine a super-secret mission yo... to undertake in Kani Cove; or ev... write a poem about your den. A... you're **not sure what to write ab**... throughout these pages we've o... some cool suggestions so you can **let your imagination run wild.** So have fun and happy writing, Jammer!

write a letter to your favorite alpha.

GET ON BOARD!